I'm Ruby

Don't Forget I'm a Princess Now

Ruby Burgess

CHAPTER 1

TEDDY

The days of 2nd and 3rd June 2022 were the worse two days of my life. I've lost humans who I love dearly but this was sheer pain I've never felt before and still feel today. You see, Teddy wasn't "just a dog", to be honest no dog is "just a dog" but Teddy was different, he was unique, a one off. Everyone who met him was charmed by him, and to be fair those who hadn't met him were too.

With thousands of followers on Facebook all over the world, and people wanting and arranging to meet him, many crying when they did. So Teddy was like I said, unique. He was beautiful inside and out, even people with their own dogs said that he was the most gorgeous and best looking dog they had ever seen. He was definitely noticeable, from his lion like hair to his babby in his gob, it wasn't long before he got comments when we were out. Many stopped us in the streets to talk to him, many nearly crashed the car they were driving at the sight of this beautiful dog carrying the most massive sloth in his mouth! Of course the sloth was a teddy bear but many had to look twice! He was strikingly handsome, so gorgeous that he was often mistaken for a girl, so beautiful I was told so many times to enter him into

Crufts. I've not met anyone who loves dogs that didn't fall for him, that didn't want to take a photo, that didn't say how striking he was.

With Teddy what you saw was what you got, cheeky, cuddly, always cute and sometimes stubborn, but always a "likkle bugga!" It was funny because most of the time he was cheeky, he got away with oh so many things and had that gorgeous smile on his face that you had to laugh at him, he certainly charmed people when we met them due to his cheekiness and had them in stitches laughing at him. He was definitely his true self and they saw him as he always was.

I've never known where anyone had to apologise to a dog for the dog actually being in the wrong, but oh yes, I did! Many times! The few times he was naughty and I had to tell him off he really didn't like it; how could the beautiful Ted be in the wrong? Well believe me sometimes he was and I'd end up apologising to him for it "onest I did!" He was funny because once he knew he was in bother he used to make it so I couldn't ignore him, he'd walk in front of me and block my way and when that didn't work, he would start tapping me with his little paw and the taps would get more frequent and slightly harder till I looked at him, then he'd do his speciality and wrap his front paws round my arm. So he was up on two legs and I had no choice but to forgive him and stroke that tummy, while apologising to him for telling him off!! It was worth it afterwards when he covered me in big sloppy kisses, you really couldn't be mad with him at all for long he just had that cheekiness that couldn't be ignored.

He had lots of letters, cards and presents come through the post for him too, most days they'd be something come for him. It was funny one day as he got a letter and all the envelope read was "Teddy Burgess face book dog", what made me laugh was that Royal mail had written on the envelope "the address is ...." and actually wrote the address on for them! He used to love looking out for the postie and if it was our regular postie he would always fuss Ted and give him a letter or parcel in his mouth which he'd trot off into the room and try to open it, even if it wasn't for him. He especially got spoiled on Valentines Day, Easter, his adoption day and of course his Birthday and Christmas. He had loads of babbies bought him {for those who don't know, his babbies were his teddy bears} and at one point he had over a 100 so what we did was, every so often we'd have a clear out and some of the older ones were donated to charity to make room for the newer ones. Each babbie had its own name too and he loved each and every one of them, sometimes having trouble deciding which one to take out for his walk. I'm sure at some point each one will have gone out with him or away with him for his olibobs. He always took one to bed with him too and would rest his head on it unless he decided to sprawl out and take up half the bed. Haha talking of that, many times I was already in bed and when it came to Andy getting in, I used to hear "come on Ted let me in" and after a minute or so of Ted not moving and not letting him in, Andy was on the edge of the bed {like me} while Ted must have had the biggest grin on his face all sprawled out in comfort.

He had so many nicknames but as you all know he was commonly known as sausage. Other nicknames were likkle bugga, likkle lad {though he said he was a "reet big lad"} Tedster, and for some reason later in life I started calling him "peaches" don't ask me why but it sort of suited him and it was between me and him, we didn't tell anyone else. But he was more known as said, affectionately as sausage and so many people called it him and he did answer to it as well. Sometimes he'd look at me all lovingly as though he was saying "I'm ya likkle sausage aren't I mummy?" I swear if any dog could talk it would be him. He knew every word we ever said to him he was so intelligent. I researched into him being a therapy dog as he would have been so good at it with his caring and gentle nature, unfortunately his epilepsy put paid to that and they wouldn't accept him. Such a shame as I know so many more people would have got so much joy from him. He would also have loved all the sausages he got for a treat for being a reet gud lad!

One thing he did love was his treats, mainly obviously sausages but for dog treats he loved gravy bones and most others, if we went out for a few hours we would take treats with us but one thing he really loved was raw carrot. We started taking that out with us as it was better for him and helped to lose some excess weight he gained with his medication and get him down to his normal healthy weight. Of course if we offered him sausage, he would snub the carrot, it's like offering a child a chocolate bun or a carrot, you know what they'd choose. The treats he absolutely loved more than anything was his advent calendars each Christmas which we filmed him opening and all his followers loved to watch the videos, he really did play to the camera too, he loved it and always made an entrance jumping off the settee and coming into the kitchen when I called his name. He would sit nicely for the first one and for the second and third he would parade round showing off and act up for the camera. One time he hit one of the calendars so hard with his paw he destroyed it and all the treats fell to the floor, he wasn't very happy when I picked them up and put them back in the calendar. Oh sausage!

He was really popular with other dogs too when we took him out for walks, he had a big group of friends on the field who all loved him and if we went anywhere different, he would join in playing with other dogs like they were old friends. There was only ever two dogs who didn't like him, both female, I told him they were jealous that they weren't his girlfriend, funny though as he never reacted back to them when they barked at him or tried to get to him, he looked as though he was saying "HUFF you know what you can do". His best friend was Spike from next door, he'd had a few good friends who had passed away and now he had teamed up with Spike, he even taught him to walk round with a babby in his mouth, which Spike still does now.

Other than being on his olibobs, Ted's favourite places were anywhere with fields and grass he could run on and roll in, and basically anywhere I was. He loved the bed too, and the settee, sprawled out all comfy showing off that tummy to get one of his rubs and then he'd clutch my hand with his paws and fall asleep, it was one of the sweetest things he ever did. He gave the best cuddles, and kisses. I loved it when I was cleaning up and would bend down to sweep the muck into the dustpan and he'd come up and just give me the loveliest kiss for no reason other than he loved me. I'd tell him I loved him too, very very much and kiss his little nose 5 times. He was always very affectionate and loved a fuss.

He'd sometimes kiss his fans {fans, supporters, followers, not sure what to call them really but they were all Team Teddy] when he met them and they'd be thrilled that they had gotten a kiss from the Yorkshire sausage. It really is amazing how many people loved him and their reaction to him when they met him. I know many people now that hadn't had the chance to meet him were very upset, especially when we had two holidays planned and had some meet ups arranged. Those holidays never happened unfortunately.

One thing's for sure though ....

WE LOVE YOU SAUSAGE

CHAPTER 2

BLACKPOOL [get your tissues]

Teddy's epilepsy was getting worse. The seizures were getting more frequent and he was having them in clusters. We had exhausted all medication avenues on where to go and what to do, he was on the maximum dosage of all he could be on. Never did we think for a moment this would be the way it went; we knew we would lose him to this god awful condition but certainly not yet and definitely not for a good few years.

We were having the best time in Blackpool, Teddy was true to form and charming everyone, those we knew and those we didn't. We'd done a few meet ups and he was making people laugh with his antics, even jumping over a small wall when he recognised Joan who we meet most times we are in Blackpool. We really laughed at that, and he had the biggest cheekiest smile on his face. We went places on the tram which he loved and made sure he got on first pushing past everyone to get the best seat, mind you, the people he pushed past were trying to push in anyway so he did us a favour. We had pub meals and he always ended up with a sausage or some of our dinner then was cheeky enough to stand at a hot dog vendor and wait there staring at us till we bought him another sausage.

We were having the best week and Teddy really was having the time of his life. We did so many things that week and we had more meet ups to do, one of them being with Ted's old mate Dexter, a fellow Springer Spaniel he had met a few times previously and they liked each other and enjoyed playing. We met Dexter, his mum Janet and our friend Sheila on Fleetwood beach on the Wednesday and I've genuinely never seen Teddy enjoy himself as much. He never was a dog that was interested in the water, he'd go out in the rain and loved it, but on the beach, he'd paddle at best and get his paws wet but he wouldn't go in the water and play. This day though he was up for it and more than happy to be in the water and get himself absolutely soaked through and have fun. We were throwing pebbles for them to chase when they saw them splash in the water. It made me cry as he was so so happy, he was always happy but there was something different about him this day. He was effortlessly running in and out of the water, jumping, dancing almost. He really let go and had the most fun with Dexter. After they'd had a play, we walked down to the café where we all got a warm drink. Storm had a toastie and I got Ted and Dexter a sausage each which didn't last either of them long. After this we went for a walk down the path at the back of the beach and Ted was off his lead, he kept sniffing at Janets bag for treats and the more we laughed at his cheekiness the cheekier he got, tapping the bag as he toddled behind Janet, to the point he was almost jogging at the side of her pulling on the bag, we were all in hysterics but it worked, he got more treats.

It was so lovely to finally see him in the sea, we were talking about it all day and night. We went to the Hotel bar that night like we always did, we stayed at the usual Hotel that we go to each visit with Julie and Steve who have also become friends, a lovely brother and sister who have ran the Hotel for over 30 years. Ted was shattered and slept most of the time in the bar on the settee and we had to wake him to go to bed. We took him out for his last wee of the night and he livened up and wanted to go for a walk so we took him quickly over the road to the top of the beach for a quick run. Once back at the hotel we settled down for the night.

It was around 6am on the Thursday when Ted either fell or jumped off the bed, we heard him land on the floor [it wasn't unusual around this time when it was getting light for him to jump off the bed and lie on the floor]. Only this time when we checked on him, he was having a seizure. I got his rescue medication [Diazepam] straight away and gave it to him, he came out of the seizure but it did take him longer than usual when he'd the medication. We spoke to him and tried to comfort him but as soon as he was out of the seizure he went straight into another one. We were allowed to use the Diazepam 3 times in half an hour so I gave him the second one and again it took him a while to come out of it. This time he started walking round the room, leaning his head on the wall, staggering as he wasn't steady on his legs and his eyes looked glazed over. Then seizure 3 happened. We were worried, it was only 6.30 in the morning and the vets wasn't open, the nearest emergency vet was 35 minutes away and there was no way we could move him in the state he was in, he was a mess.

This carried on until 7.45 and by now he'd had 15 seizures. I was hysterical. Andy wanted to try to carry Ted downstairs as he had stopped fitting but was all motionless, we were now able to safely move him, [hoping he wouldn't seizure again while moving him and getting him to the vet]. We had wrapped him in a blanket for easiness. We rushed downstairs and saw Steve who had heard the commotion upstairs but obviously didn't know what was happening. We got Ted to the car and laid him on the back seat, he wasn't moving, his eyes were glazed, nothing behind them. He really wasn't well. We rushed him to the vets which was 7 or 8 minutes away [it was vets for pets which was his actual vets back home] so they should be able to get all his information up. They weren't open for another hour but I ran and banged on the door of the shop louder than I've done anything. Someone opened the door and I don't know how they understood me in my panic but I was pointing to the car. Two nurses came running out with a stretcher type thing and lifted Ted onto it and took him inside. We followed in a panic and gave all the information we could and luckily, they got his medical history up from our own vets.

The vet wasn't due in work till 9.30 but the nurses sedated Ted and did what they needed to do then rang the vet to come in early to attend to him. We were talking to the nurses when the vet dashed in, not long after she was called so she made good time. We were told to leave him and they would call us as soon they could with any news. I won't lie, I half thought we would lose him but I wasn't ready to let him go and told them no matter what the cost, save my boy. Reluctantly we made our way back to the hotel, we had been told that someone would be with Ted all the time and he wouldn't be left alone at all.

We had arrangements that day to meet Jane and Simon, two friends we also met on each occasion we were in Blackpool. I rang Jane and told her what had happened and said we wouldn't now be meeting them due to not having Ted. Jane rang back later and asked if they could still see us as she had something for us so we said we would meet them at our hotel at 12 noon which we did. While talking they suggested we go for a drink to pass the time on and try to occupy our minds so we went to the pub for a soft drink and passed a few hours. The vet had rang a few times and said Ted was holding his own but they are keeping him sedated for now. Apparently, all the staff had fell in love with him and were all wanting to sit with him. One nurse sat with him while eating her dinner as she didn't want to leave him.

The rest of the day was awful, waiting for the phone to ring which it did at 4pm, by this time I was confident he would be ok but the call wasn't what we wanted or expected. Ted unfortunately needed more treatment and this vet practise was closing at 5pm so we had to take him to the emergency vet at Preston which was the one we were trying to get him to that morning but we weren't able to move him due to the cluster of seizures. We picked him up from the vets and thanked them for what they had done, they had sedated him for the journey and we were all hoping he didn't have another turn in the car. Two lovely nurses brought him out to the car on a stretcher covered in a blanket and they both cried saying goodbye to him and said how adorable he was.

The vets had rang the emergency vet to expect us so they could take him straight in and start treating him, on arrival two people came out and carried him from the car into the building. We were left for what seemed like ages in reception until a vet came to see us. I begged him and begged him to save him, we were told it didn't look good, from a quick examination he said it looked like his brain had swollen from the fits. They took our details and told us they'd ring us; we had to leave him and make our way back. That night was awful, we decided to go downstairs in the bar to socialise to pass the time I suppose, I dunno really, we just needed that phone call and waiting for it was torture. Should we wait in our room? Should we be with others and pass time? What do you do? I don't suppose there was any right or wrong answer but that damned phone didn't ring.

I rang them at 9.30 to see what was happening and they said they had been trying to contact me but somehow, they missed a digit out of my number and couldn't get in touch. Why didn't I ring earlier? I thought no news is good news and they had worked a miracle. Or was I dreading the worst? I don't know what was going through my head, can you imagine how we felt? Not only what had happened but to happen on your holiday in a different city? To take your beloved pet away and it ends like this? People can judge if they want, but put yourself in my shoes, actually you wouldn't want to as you're probably crying already. I felt every bad emotion that day, anger, bitterness, upset, pissed off, did I mention anger? Yes, I was angry, I was angry this could happen to my boy, this boy loved by how many thousands around the world, never hurt anyone or anything and this is what comes. The phone call wasn't nice, Ted had unfortunately had another 16 seizures while at the vets, once they brought him out of one, he had another, and another. They said they were going to keep him a few more hours and keep trying but we had to prepare for the worse.

We went back to our room, we didn't want everyone else brought down by our sadness, it was their holiday too with their own dogs. Storm wanted to go back to her own room which was across the hall from us and she left her door open in case we needed to wake her.

We laid on the bed, we didn't sleep, we didn't speak, we didn't look at each other, we didn't know what to say, we didn't know what to do. Then the call came at 12.00 midnight and it was the worst thing they could have said to me, we need to go to say goodbye. I told them to please keep working on him till we get there, don't let him go, please, please save him. The drive to Preston was awful, it was quiet, the only noise was the sobs we were making. I was still half thinking they'd be able to save him and we could bring him home. I wasn't ready to lose him, none of us were. We arrived at the vets and went to reception and it was about 5 minutes before a vet came out, he told us all the 3 vets on duty had a discussion and all agreed it was the kindest thing to do to let him go, the only thing to do.

We were taken into the room to see him and was surprised to see Ted was awake, they had brought him out of sedation so we could say goodbye. As soon as he saw us his little face lit up and he smiled, his tail wagged and kept wagging. He looked beautiful as always. He tried to stand up to get to us but his legs had gone, they gave way on him. I laid down with him on the floor and hugged him, held his paw, stroked his tummy, he kissed me licking my face, I kissed his little nose so many times and smothered his oh so beautiful face with more kisses. Storm and Andy had a cuddle with him and gave him a kiss then sat back and let me have time with him, I was the closest person to him and they knew through their own grief what he meant to me and what I meant to him. I was talking to him and loving him when the nurse came in who was looking after him and said he's likely to have another seizure anytime soon and that will be when the vet comes in. I was holding and cuddling him so tight, his little paws cuddling me. We had about 15 minutes with him when the worst happened and he started to seizure again, I screamed, I shouted, I screamed again, I knew this was the last one he would ever have and that we were losing him. He was brought out of the seizure and put back into sedation, the vet said it was time, I held him tighter and closer than ever, I begged and begged, please do something else, anything, save him we can't lose him, please!! The vet said if I gave him a million pounds now to save him it wouldn't work, it wouldn't make a difference, it wouldn't change anything, his brain had gone, his legs had gone, his body had given up. Ted had suffered 34 seizures in 24 hours something they'd never seen before. I was hysterical, screaming, howling, laid on the floor with him begging him to stand up and walk out. I've never felt so empty, so sick, so sad.

I was on the floor for what seemed an eternity, screaming and not caring who heard, this was the hardest thing I've ever had to do. We had to decide what we wanted to do with Teddy, obviously we wanted our baby back, I paid for him to be taken away and cremated. He would be sent by courier back to our house where he belonged in a week or so. We chose a lovely wooden casket for his ashes.

Teddy passed away at 2.45 on the 3rd of June 2022 with a massive smile on his face like only Teddy could.

I did think if we hadn't gone away on holiday would he still be here? If we hadn't taken him to the beach and let him go in the water, would he still be here? He was so happy that day like he knew somehow it was going to be the last day of his life and he was going to damned well enjoy it. Everyone says if he was going to go then he would have gone regardless of where we were but I think maybe the excitement of that day triggered something quicker than it should have and brought the seizures on. To this day I still wonder if we were at home would it have happened? We'll never know but it's something that haunts me and I wonder if we would still have him now. We always knew the seizures would take him, never ever did I think they'd take him so cruelly and so young. Age 7 is not old for any breed of dog, especially a Springer and he should have had many more years with us.

I do appreciate and know that he had the best life and couldn't have been any happier than he was but it's little comfort watching him have to leave us the way he did. If love would keep him alive, he'd be around for many years.

We cut our holiday short as we couldn't stay without him, Julie and Steve at the hotel were amazing and also felt our grief, they obviously love dogs and they felt very sad this had happened while we were staying with them. They were absolutely distraught and cried their own tears. The other guests staying there were all very nice and sympathetic. It was truly just awful what had happened. These were the worst two days of my life; I've been through much pain and heartbreak but this was on another level. Also Reece didn't know, he had by choice stayed home so we had to leave to break the news to him which obviously was hard for us and him.

We also broke the news to Spike and his dad, they saw us arrive home and get out of the car, we were home a day early and they knew something was wrong, then they saw us walk in the house crying, without Ted. We also told the neighbours at the other side to us who also loved Ted, there wasn't a dry eye amongst us. Reece had pre-arranged to go out that night, obviously we weren't supposed to be home, he had plans with his friends. We told him to still go, there was nothing he could do now, we'd just be sat crying.

I cried each day, I woke up crying, I feel asleep crying, I cried in between, I cried all day, non-stop. I didn't eat, I didn't really talk to anyone, except to say I missed my baby, my boy, my sausage.

It's broke me writing this so I'm leaving it here, I'm sure you're crying with me. Have a break now, put the kettle on, have a tipple, wipe your eyes. I know in the time since we have lost Ted, you've all cried your own tears and we thank you for your lovely support.

Teddy: We love you; you were a one off, there'll never be another like you and we'll never forget you, we'll keep your memory alive. TEDDY WE LOVE YOU 7.3.2015-3.6.2022

CHAPTER 3

I NEED A DOG

The house was empty, it was awful, it was quiet and felt so cold and well, empty without Ted. When we lost our beautiful Roxy, we still had Ted and though losing her was very hard and we miss her so much, we focused on Ted. When we lost Ted we had no other dog, we were so used to having a dog 24/7 we really didn't know what to do. He was with us full time; we didn't leave him alone due to the epilepsy so everywhere we went he came too. So when you've had years of never being without a dog at your side it's a huge loss. Any dog or any animal / pet is a huge loss of course but we never got a break from Ted, not that we wanted one.

Me and Andy were discussing what we wanted to do, rescue another dog now or wait a while. The fact we'd hardly left the house in a few weeks made us decide its best to maybe at least start looking.

We'd been to the garden centre a few times to make Ted's memorial garden but other than that we'd not been out or really done anything and we realised how much of your life, in a good way a dog does take up. We could get up in the morning and go for a walk, but what would be the point without a dog? And how long before we bump into someone we know with their own dog?

Someone who knew Ted and didn't know the sad news? We didn't want to, and knew we couldn't replace Teddy, that's the last thing we wanted to do, but we needed a dog, another dog in need that we could love and could hopefully love us too.

We saw on the Springer Spaniel website where Teddy was adopted from that there was an elderly girl called Ruby who needed a foster home as she had been puppy farmed and was quite frankly in a mess.

Ruby needed a foster home as she was needing several surgeries and it wasn't nice for any dog to recover in kennels let alone an older girl who hadn't had, by the sounds of it had a nice life up to now.

We spoke about it and decided to foster Ruby until she was well enough to go to her permanent home [yes, I know we're crap fosterers haha].

There were a few questions we asked ourselves if we could do this so soon after losing Ted.

Could we love another dog? We would certainly try but she's only on foster right ?........ and we're looking after her and helping her through surgeries more than loving her. Obviously, we'll care for her and do what she needs and yes, we'll no doubt end up loving her but if we're going be foster carers we need to think more about her health and getting her better. It also helps she's a girl; I think a boy right now would be harder as Ted's my boy and a damned hard act to follow.

Could we do all the regular vets visits after what we went through with Teddy?........ Yes, it's a different vets to where Teddy was registered so we don't have to see the usual ones.

Could we spend weeks sleeping on the settee even though we had just ordered a new mattress for the bed and won't be able to sleep on it for weeks?........ Yes, if Ruby could sleep on the streets for a chunk of her life and in a small hard cage, we could sleep on the settee for as long as she needed us to.

Could we take her for walks to the same places we took Ted and face seeing his friends for the first time without him? …. We have to do it sometimes so why not now?

So shall we meet her? …….. Yes!

We made an appointment with Heather from the rescue who saw Ted's adoption through with us [and who we keep in touch with and donate money to regularly] for 11.00am on Sunday the 19th of June to meet Ruby.

We knew she wasn't the prettiest dog from pictures we had seen on the website but that tugged at us even more and made us want to make a difference to her life. In the pictures she looked so sad and so fragile that we were all the more determined to bring her home and do what we could to get this girl a new home.

We aimed to bring her home and foster her while another dog could take Ruby's rescue space. Once Ruby was better and all fixed, we would foster another dog and so on. It's like helping two dogs really as Ruby would free up a rescue space for another dog to be looked after. That way it's a win win, and Ruby would eventually find her new home and new family.

Only it didn't quite turn out like that, did it?

CHAPTER 4

FROM THE CAGE TO THE STREETS

Hello! I'm Ruby ...
[not quite a Princess yet]

My back story isn't pretty, it isn't a happy one or a good one and to be honest with you I want to forget about it. But I do need to tell you what happened to me and this is my happy ending where I'm loved, wanted and cared for. At some point I ended up in rescue after I was found wondering the streets in Barnsley, I've no idea how long I was on the streets for, I've no idea what I did wrong to end up on the streets, I've no idea how I survived, but I did and lucky for me I was found by the stray dog wardens who safely captured me and got me to safety. I know they shaved all my fur off because it was all mattered and I was covered in my own mess, which I'd most probably laid in. I had lumps and bumps all over me [more of that in another chapter] but all I was bothered about was I was safe now, probably for the first time in my life.

You see, I was used for breeding, or puppy farming for another term, it seems once I had given them the puppies they needed to sell and made money out of me,

I was no longer wanted or needed. I never had anyone to call my own human, I was bred and abused. I was trapped in a cage most of my life and that shows even now as I spin around a lot. When you're in a cage there's not an awful lot of space, you can't go forward, you can't go backwards, you can't go sideways, the only place to go really is round and around, I only ever spin one way I don't spin the other way. My new family have tried to get me to spin the other way but I'm a stubborn mare and like to go to the right, when I spin they call me Kylie and say I'd look good in gold hotpants …. "I'm spinning around get out of my way" hahaha, we do laugh. [I can laugh now because it's all in fun and I've left all that cruelty behind me]

Anyway, I had lots of puppies and even more puppies, I know they'd be absolutely beautiful because I mean, look at me I'm the prettiest most gorgeous girl you ever did see. [Apparently, I wasn't but I've bloomed in to a right beauty]. When the puppies were old enough, they were taken away from me and sold, you know how it works so I'm not going to explain it all but puppy farming is cruel and when your exposed to it it's even worse. What if I loved my puppies and wanted to keep them? Or what if I didn't want puppies to begin with? That choice wasn't mine and was taken away from me and after all that I was dumped! Dumped on the streets and left to fend for myself, they never cared about me, they didn't care about my puppies. I was left having to find a safe place to sleep so I wasn't hurt by someone in the night, having to find every scrap of food regardless of what it was just so I could survive, having to watch every single minute of every single day to keep myself safe. What had I done to deserve this? I gave them puppies, I made them money, then I come to this! Is this the life of every dog? Do we all live like this? Because I'll tell you something, this isn't living, its existing, surviving, fighting, don't I deserve more? What have I done wrong?

Are all dogs treated like this? Is it just me? Why aren't I wanted? Why am I lonely? I only want another dog to bark at, to play with, to pinch food off – I mean share food with. All I see around me are what seem like lucky dogs on leads with humans and I really want a human of my own, I want to be loved , I want to be stroked, I want to be fed, I want to be taken for walks, I want to feel the comfiness of a bed not a hard closed cage or the hard pavement of the street or the wet muddy grass when I'm trying to sleep. I want a family of my own, a human, maybe a mummy and daddy, maybe some little humans, maybe another dog to play with.

One day as I said, I was found by the stray dog warden and when they had shaved my fur and to an extent, cleaned me up, I was taken to a rescue centre, only at that time I didn't know it was rescue. There was lots of other dogs there, mainly Springer Spaniels like me so I thought this was it, this is my home now. I was happy as we got all got treated so well, a nice warm place to live and nice blankets and beds to sleep, we did have to share but I didn't even mind that as I'd never had a blanket before, never had a bed before and more importantly I was safe. I had company too with the other dogs though I found it hard to join in as I didn't know how to play. I'd not had a ball to chase before, or a toy to play with and I didn't really know what to do. We had lovely humans come to see us too, they fed us and for the first time in my life I went out on a lead and had a proper walk, I can't tell you how that felt, it was a feeling I've never known, oh go on then I will tell you how it felt, blooming wonderful!!! So wonderful I did my spin round every time I saw them, especially when they were feeding me. No more scrounging in bins, no more eating off the floor, no more fighting for every morsal I could get, I was fed food, proper dog food and sometimes we had human meat! I don't mean we ate humans haha, don't be silly, I think even I'd turn my nose up at that, I mean meat that humans eat, chicken, beef, liver, sausages that sort of thing, oooh it were lovely.

I'd settled at the kennels where the rescue was, like I say everyone was so lovely and I had other dogs around me and I thought this was my life now, I was happy, but I kept seeing some dogs leave and they never came back. I know when they were leaving, they had humans with them cuddling them and taking them to a car where they drove off. Now I'm thinking, is there life after here? Is there more out there? Would I ever get that chance? I did secretly cross my little paws and dream of what could only be a forever home but I knew I was safe and happy and fed [yes, I like my food] so I could like it here if no one ever wanted me.

I was treated really well and had lots of love and fuss from the people who worked and volunteered at the kennels. I had lots of vets visits too and tests done that I'd never had before so that was all new. It seemed like it was all for my own good though and someone was finally caring for me and looking after me even if I did have the thermometer shoved up my you know whaty me bobby boo [bum bum] when I went to the vets. How very dare they!

It seems I would need a few surgeries at the vets and to have these surgeries I needed to be out of kennels and in a home so I could recuperate, as kennels weren't any place for an older girl like to me to be even though I get treated amazing. I needed to be with someone all day and night to look after me and help my recovery so the rescue put my photo on their website. They were appealing for someone to take me but they had to be dedicated and experienced, to have time on their hands to look after me, to take me for various vets visits and that sounded like a hard task so I did keep my little paws crossed. The write up on me was honest, I was an older girl, 10+ and needed spaying, as well as two mammary strips, and it was likely I'd have other health issues too that needed to be faced with any potential adoptee / fosterer. Let's face it, my chances didn't look good.

As written previously [not by me, keep that noted] I wasn't the prettiest looking girl [more of this later too] so that was against me too. But there must be someone out there daft enough and crazy enough to want sleepless nights and the love of an old girl. I won't ask for much. Food, I like my food!

CHAPTER 5

I'M RUBY
{You can now call me Princess]

It was what I thought was a normal day when all my life changed forever, never did I think in a world of Princess's that I'd fall and land on my furry little paws. It's not unusual [who am I? Tom Jones] on any day at the kennels to have lots of people around and for dogs to have visitors. This particular day I was minding my own business after I'd been fed and looking at all the other dogs who were getting their meal taken to them wishing I could have some more, [I do like my food] I was looking around and noticed two humans waiting round. I looked to see if they had food, they didn't. The lady human was fussing the other dogs and being all silly, the male human was stood looking round, trying to avoid the lady human who was quite loud going "ooooh you are gorgeous" to every dog she got close to. I did wonder what was going off when they came over to the paddock myself and other dogs were in. The lady human was looking at the dogs saying how gorgeous they were and then she pointed to me and said something, the male nodded, they never said I was gorgeous though, why? How did they find every other Springer gorgeous and not me? And what had she said to the man about me? I was taken out of the paddock and they came over to me, the man had hold of my lead, the lady sat on the floor at the side of me. The kennel staff were still feeding other dogs that had just come back from their walk and I wanted more food. What's this silly woman doing sat on the floor at side of me for when she's got no food? Well I'm not interested, no food, no interest.

They didn't give up though, she was sat there ages talking to me and stroking me when all of a sudden I actually had a thought. Are they taking me? Taking me home? Could they? Could they really? Will they feed me? Now I don't know what was said but I know they were talking to the kennel lady who looked after me mostly and then there I was, walking out of the kennels on a lead. Was this it? Was this my big moment? I walked at the side of them and then I saw a car, a car like I'd seen other dogs jump in and never come back to the kennels. I half clumsily jumped; half had what I hoped my was new daddy lift me in the back seat of the car. What I hope is my new mummy sat at the side of me. Is this my lucky day? Is it? Is it really? The lady was loving me and stroking me and saying, "its ok sweetheart, its ok".

I never knew what to expect but what I didn't expect was to be driven to more kennels, another rescue! Now what's happening? I'm not going to a different kennels, really, I'm not, I don't want to and I won't. I snuggle up to the lady and she cuddles me, I feel safe but I'm still unaware what's happening. Then I see someone coming to the car, she gets in, she turns round and sees me and screams, and shrieks, crikey this human girl is louder than that human lady when she was gushing over the

28

other dogs. I think the human girl likes me though so I climb over the back seat to sit on her knee on the front seat and she's crying, she's happy, well if she's happy how the blazers does she think I feel? I think it's happened; I think I found my family; I think I'm going to get fed. Well I know I've found them cus I'm darned if I'm going back now, I tell you what, I think I've landed on my little furry paws after all. Oh, the reason I got taken to the other kennels? Turns out the human girl, Storm volunteers at a different animal rescue and we were picking her up from work, phewwww they not dropping me off!

I was made to go back on the back seat for my own safety but I didn't mind as I still got cuddles. I've not been in the back seat of a car before so I was sat up, looking out of the window, looking at the people walking by, looking at the dogs on leads and feeling smug thinking hopefully that will me soon. I took everything in, the fresh air from the open windows, the smells from the open windows, the laughter of children from the open windows. I didn't want to miss a thing; this was hopefully the start of a new life for me and I want to savour each moment. We pulled up outside a house and I got helped out of the car, I was so excited that when I tried to get out myself, I ended up in a tizzy. So this is it, my big moment, the best moment of my life, wait for it, I'm up the steps, I'm in the porch, I'm in the house and they are all fussing me. I've not even got space to do a celebratory spin round because they're all over me and I'm happy, I mean I'm really really happy. They do give me a bit of space after to explore and that's when I go in to spin mode and I spin and I spin and I spin! Turns out there's a human boy to meet as well, it's all so exciting. I wonder what he will make of me in my new home! What do I make of me in my new home? I think, I know, it's where I'm supposed to be, look at me, spinning round in my house, my own house!

I had a garden too, really, I did, I went out and had a look round, it was massive I had so much room to roam around in and I had my first pee pee in the garden. I'd christened it now, so it really was mine. I went back in the house, then back outside, then back in the house, I had something I'd never had before, choices. I could make my own decisions what I wanted to do and it felt so good, I even had a cheeky look upstairs! There were bedrooms for the humans and I just knew I'd make myself comfy and at home on that massive bed, ooh this will be the life. I don't think I've ever been so excited; I mean I was excited when I was rescued off the streets and taken to kennels but now this is my moment, my glory, my new life, my new home. My new forever home and no one is taking that away from me now I've landed on my fluffy furry little paws and got them well and truly under the table ... and on the settee... and on the bed / beds cus I'm quite partial to all 3 of them!

I was given my first meal there, it was what my brother [did you get that? My brother!!!!] Teddy had left, there was a box with lots of pouches of food in it and I had my first packet. Out of my own food dish, in my own food stand with my own water dish next to it. All mine. There's even water dishes in the kitchen, and outside! I was told that I'd have a water dish upstairs too in the bedroom I'll be sleeping in! They couldn't bring a food dish up too could they? I do like my food. I've never had anything that's been all mine before. I ate my food and jumped on the settee where I had my first cuddle in my new home with my new family. I was told I'd get fed each day, and I'd get dry and wet food, and I'd get treats too, I like the sound of that, treats, yum, I don't have to fight for food now, I get fed by my humans, my family, my mummy and daddy. I know I needed to be fattened up as well so that's more food in my belly.

I'm happy, I'm here, I'm home.

I'm settled, I'm loved, I'm a Princess.

Never in a world of Princess's did I think I'd be so lucky, so loved.

So here I am RUBY TRIXIE BURGESS but you can call me Princess.

CHAPTER 6

SORRY LOOKING LITTLE THING

When I was picked up from kennels, even though I was already loved, I was called a sorry looking little thing, really I was. Well that's not very nice is it? I apparently had a pretty face but wasn't in the best condition as I was shaved of all my fur, I was skinny and I was covered in lumps and bumps [more of that later] and my tail was practically down to the bone. No fur and a bendy grisly bit on the end of my tail, and it was yellow, presumably from my own mess. I stunk abit as well, so they said, I think the word they used was "ripe", "Ruby's ripe". But for now this sorry looking little thing was even more excited as I got taken to the pet shop for the first time in my life. And what did I get bought me? First thing was a bed, a nice comfy, cosy bed all for me and not to share , no more hard cages, no more hard pavements or muddy wet grass, oh no, a nice comfy bed. I parked myself down in one near enough straight away, there were some beds on the bottom shelf near the floor and I climbed in one and laid down. Apparently, I'm not supposed to fall asleep in it in the shop hehehe, well it was so comfy what else was I supposed to do? So the bed went in the trolley, it really was mine, I'll never have an uncomfortable night again. Then to the most important thing, food and treats, I do love my food, and anyone else's food really, I'm not fussy, if it's edible I'll eat it. I got lots of food put in the trolley, [because I enjoyed what I'd just eaten, what Teddy had, they bought me more of that] then on to the treats which all looked sooo nice, even nicer when they didn't know what I liked so they gave me a few samples from the pic n mix tubs. They didn't know at the time that I would eat anything and all the free treats were lovely and well, they went down a treat!

I had a new collar bought me, brand spanking new and pink [so it must mean I'm a Princess now] followed by a new matching lead. I wasn't allowed a harness yet as I had to have my surgery first and the harness would rub on my lady bitties then my scars. I could also get a coat once I was healed but luckily for now it was summer and it was warm. My new mummy [I'll come to that in a bit] said she would get me a name tag too with details on it of my new address. [I did also later in that month get a name tag saying "I'm a Princess" so now it's official]

We got home and I settled in my new bed and I had the biggest smile on my face while my new mummy was taking lots of photos of me, the sorry looking little thing. I think she secretly thought I was gorgeous. I keep saying new mummy, it seems I was on foster, they were just fostering me till I was well enough after surgeries to be adopted, but we all know how that ended don't we? Yes, they were crap, hehehe they kept me, they couldn't part with me, they fell in love with me and said I was staying forever. I'm so glad they are crap. It was nice though that a space in rescue became available for another sorry looking little thing. I've been adopted!! Me! The sorry looking little thing! Never again in a world of Princess's did I think I'd have my own family, my own home, my own bed, my own choices, my own food, my own mummy and daddy.

I'd been with my new family for a few weeks and they really thought I was deaf; I didn't react to any noises or to any times they spoke to me. I was food orientated and didn't seem to acknowledge anything else. One day I was laid in my bed and boy did I jump; I jumped all the way out of my bed and ran into the hallway. Why? There was a massive almighty bang! That's right, I heard a bang. They realised I wasn't deaf and just didn't know how to communicate, even the kennels thought I may be deaf so it had been on-going that I had no or very little hearing. It seems that most of my life I had been spoken at, not spoken to, so I had little sense of communication and this was about to change. After my family knew that I actually could hear, things got much better as even though they had spoken to me before they really started working on communicating with me and using my name when talking to me. I was starting to learn ....

"Ruby, do you want to go out for a wee wee?"

"Ruby, do you want to go out for a walk?"

"Ruby, it's bedtime sweetheart, are we going upstairs?"

"Ruby, it's dinner time" [I didn't need telling twice for that]

"Ruby, let's go out and see if you want to play"

"Ruby this, Ruby that, Ruby Ruby Ruby" [I was going to write another Ruby but if I wrote my name 4 times, you'd all burst in to song, wouldn't you?]

I loved it and learnt so much over the next few weeks as they took time to talk to me, not at me, which as I said had been the bug bear most of my life, spoken at, not to.

I was allowed to sleep on mummy and daddy's bed at night, I couldn't jump up so mummy lifted me up and I laid in between them. In the morning when I woke up and saw mummy, I always crawled up the bed for a cuddle and we'd lay for half hour while mummy tickled my tummy and stroked me. Then it was the best time of the day, breakfast! What was I having today? Mummy tried to feed me up with me being so skinny and as well as dog food I had tuna, chicken, beef and scrambled eggs. Oh and on a Sunday, get this, I had bacon and sausage, it was supposed to be daddy's but it went in my belly! I was putting weight on, now who was a sorry looking little thing?

After breakfast I was taken out for walks and I absolutely loved it, different places and different smells. I found it a bit hard at first as I loved been outside but yet I was anxious to get home just in case they changed their minds and were taking me back as I couldn't believe I was finally so lucky. For the first few weeks I just ploughed through my walks, I did sniff but I was more focused on getting to where I was going so I could get back home. I'd just look straight in front of me and aim at the path I was on. It took me a while to actually "be a dog" and actually do what a dog, what a Springer should do, explore and enjoy my walks with my family.

I was meeting some of Teddy's friends too, if I went on the field, I would see a dog who played with Ted, but you see I don't know to play, I've never been taught and even though mummy and daddy did try to play with balls and stuff with me, I shown no interest at all. It seemed to be too late to teach an old dog new tricks, though they really did try and perserverd with me. When other dogs tried to play with me, I just stood there and let them sniff me and walk round me and they seemed a bit miffed I wasn't joining in. At this time I was on an extra-long lead so I had the choice to play or run, or go which ever way I wanted to but I just stood there. Mummy and daddy did a little run to try to get me to join in and I did a little trot through the grass, they did laugh and say I looked cute, funny that, I thought I was a sorry looking little thing. Most people tried to get me to join in with them, tried to help me play, I just wanted a fuss and a stroke, oh and a treat if they had one or two in their pockets? Please? I do like my food and I'd never turn down a treat.

Everyone that met me loved me, they were told all about my sad story and previous life and about me having puppies. They were told about how I was found roaming the streets and how I came to be in rescue. They were told how mummy and daddy lost Ted and how uncannily I ended up in rescue that very same day Ted sadly passed. They were told how it seems to be fate that as Ted left, I appeared, like it was a sign I was going to be taken home and adopted. As though Teddy knew I needed a new happy life and he left so I could get my new family. They all said they're so glad I've got a happy ending but they're not half as glad as I am let me tell you!

We did many new things I'd not done before, even just sitting outside on the back garden in the sun, or the shade, I didn't mind which. I'd sit, or lay, and look at the birds in the trees, listen to them singing, watch them flap their wings fighting to get into the bird house for food. I'd watch the cats in the garden waiting for the birds, trying to catch them. I'd watch daddy gardening or watch mummy picking up leaves off Teddy's Garden and say some naughty words when it wasn't as tidy as she'd like it to be. I'd listen at the dogs over the fence barking, apparently Teddy used to join in and bark back at them, I wasn't bothered, I just liked listening to different sounds while I watched the world go by.

People came to the house to meet me, all saying not only how lucky I am, knowing that my family would love me unconditionally, but also telling me how beautiful and gorgeous I am.

Sorry looking little thing?

Who? Me?

CHAPTER 7

LUMPS, BUMPS N GETTING THE HUMP

A few days before, I'd had the most amazing time on my first ever proper day out but more of that later. I'd already been told at this point that I'd been adopted and my family were keeping me which made it easier knowing I was having surgery and going back to my forever home. I was having my first mammary strip and was being spayed along with having my lumps and bumps removed. As well as lumps on my side and belly I also had what they affectionately called a blueberry on my neck. It was a lump and looked, well like a blueberry and though it was "cute" it needed to come off.

I was dropped off at the vets at 8.45 and taken straight into the back to prep for surgery while mummy and daddy signed the forms of consent and spoke to the nurse. When they left the vets, I could hear mummy crying, well good! How the blazers did she think I felt?? I knew it was for the best but I tell you I wasn't looking forward to it and hoped I'd at least get some nice food for tea when I'm allowed home. All the vets, nurses and staff were really lovely and helped me settle and keep me calm. They were so lovely to me all through the day but I couldn't wait to get home.

I was so happy when I saw mummy and daddy waiting for me after the surgery. They'd already been to see the vet for them to explain what I'd had done. I'd had one side mammary strip and I'd been spayed so no more puppies and I'd had my lumps including my blueberry removed. I was taken to the waiting room where I saw mummy and daddy and well, did I go crackers!! Mummy screeched ... "aww baby, mummy's little girl you're so brave look at your little baby gro, how cute do you look?" and I span and I span and I span. I wasn't supposed to spin, I had to be as still as I could cos of my stitches but I was so excited to go home. Daddy had to lift me in and out of the car, and up the steps to the house. I was more interested in my tea, what was I having? The vet had apparently given me a few tins of bland food so it didn't upset my belly but tomorrow I could have proper food and mummy said I could have tuna and scrambled eggs, not together though, mind you I wouldn't have minded, it all goes in the same hole don't it? And I'm not fussy, I do like my food.

We slept downstairs that night, I was on the settee at the side of mummy cus once I was asleep, I didn't move so I was safe. I had to go back to the vets every few days to have a check-up and they were really pleased with me, the biggest problem was my baby gro. If I needed a wee it needed to be unclipped and folded back so I wouldn't wet it, I did have a few accidents so in the end mummy left it unclipped but made sure my poorly scars were covered up but to be fair to myself I was really clever and never went near them anyway, such a good clever girl.

We ended up sleeping downstairs the whole time of my recovery. Apart from keeping my baby gro dry, the worst thing was that I wasn't allowed out for walks but luckily the weather was warm and we spent most of the days outside on the back garden. I'd just lay in the shade watching what mummy and daddy were doing and they kept coming over to me for a fuss. I always had water outside too and they brought my bed out for me in case I wanted to lay in it. [I've got 3 beds now, one downstairs, one upstairs in mummy and daddy's room and one outside]

I recovered well from my first surgery but we found out that one of the lumps I had removed was cancer, luckily, they caught it all but there's no guarantee it won't come back but for now I was clear and had a few weeks free before my second surgery of mammary strip on my other side. I dread to think what could have happened if I'd not been rescued, the lump would have gone undetected, I'm shuddering at the thought of it.

I was back to my walks again; I got taken out for short walks to build my strength back up again as it had been 5 weeks since I'd been able to go out. My next surgery was booked for another few weeks which meant I wouldn't be able to go out again but I was enjoying my walks for now. Mummy washed the baby gro I had ready for the next surgery but it was tight on me, I'd put weight on, mummy said it was too much good food, I put it down to the fact I'd not been active for weeks and weeks [not my fault] and I think I was right and mummy was wrong. Last thing I wanted or needed was my food intake cutting down! I do love my food.

I was taken in for my next surgery and this one should've been so easy compared to the first one, you'd think anyway. I was dropped off at the vets like last time and left with a nurse. Mummy didn't cry this time cus she knew I'd be ok [what is she? A vet? How in the world of all Princess's did she know I'd be ok?] I felt better last time when I heard her howling....

Again surgery went well and I was allowed home, this time though I had the right hump! I couldn't get out of the vets fast enough. I half ran to the car and tried to jump in before daddy could lift me up. Mummy tried to get in the back seat with me and I sprawled out so far there wasn't enough room so she had to sit in the front. Mummy tried talking to me but I put my head down and stared in front of me, I just wasn't interested in what she had to say, I just wanted to get home. I tried to jump out of the car when we got home but daddy got to me first and lifted me out, he also lifted me up the steps and when he put me down in the front porch, I headed straight into the door before it was unlocked, not a good idea cus now I've banged my head. I had my lead taken off me and I got straight in my bed, yes, I had the right hump on. I didn't even want a love, fuss or hug off mummy and apart from food, they are my favourite things.

When I woke up, I saw food in my dish, white fish, one of my favourites cooked in milk and mashed up, yum. But then I remembered I'd got the hump on so I refused to eat it while they were watching and trying to encourage me. After a while they went in the kitchen so it was my chance to eat up and I ate all the lovely fish while they were out of the room and scurry back to bed before they saw me. When they came back in, they saw the empty dish and said I was a good girl for eating up and gave me a stroke on my head. I slept in my bed all that night and didn't even get up for a wee. Mummy said if I had an accident in bed she would just wash it with my baby gro. Mummy and daddy stayed downstairs too all through this second recovery and this was to be a long drawn out one. That next day I was happier, I got out of bed but wouldn't go out for a wee, they were worried and said if I'd not been by mid-afternoon [24 hours after surgery] they'd ring the vets. I ate my breakfast which was normal boring dog food after that lovely fish I had last night but like I say I like my food. I climbed back in bed after and didn't do much for the next few hours. Mummy and daddy were told that I could be like this but if I'd not drank or wee wee for 24 hours after the surgery, they'd have to ring back up like I said. I did eventually have a drink of water and I got out of bed and ventured outside. I just walked round the garden and all the time mummy's hoping I'd pee pee, I got the hump again, I mean who pees on demand and with people watching? I went back inside and back to bed. Around an hour before the deadline I went out on the garden and I pee peed, mummy was clapping like a seal and ran inside to tell daddy. He came out and told me I was a good girl and I did another pee pee just to him to show him how good I really was. Clever Ruby.

This time I ended up with an infection in my wound, it hindered my recovery and I was at the vets each day to have it cleaned with special ointment and a fresh dressing put on. We had to go at the end of the working vet day as I had to be the last pet they saw because the infection I had meant other animals could catch it, apparently it was the equivalent of human MRSA. Each time we went we had to stay outside and away from the pets in the surgery till they had all gone then I had my treatment. Yes, I got the hump on again, I was being prodded and poked in places a lady should never be prodded or poked in. This went on for several weeks until the infection finally healed, I wasn't allowed my stitches out for a few more weeks after this though as there was one small part of the wound still slightly open though thankfully infection free. I was getting the hump quite a bit this time as not only wasn't I allowed out for walks but I wasn't allowed on the settee either this time so was confined to my bed. I wasn't allowed to jump in case I burst my stitches and by now I was getting too big to pick up.

On one of the many vets trips I finally got the stitches out, it had been a very long 8 weeks, boy was I ready to feel free again, no baby gro, no stiches and finally allowed on the settee and out for walks.

By this time I was told I could have a harness after a few weeks of the scars healing. I was also allowed back on the bed but cus mummy had to lift me up I didn't like it now, because to lift me up she was near all my scars and they were still tender so they took my bed upstairs at night and I slept in it in their room [I only had that one bed at that time not 3 like I have now]. I was also too heavy now to pick up, again due to lack of exercise by not being allowed out for walks, nothing to do with me liking my food ……..

Just when I thought all my surgeries were over, I was told I had to have my teeth done, a dental, previous tests shown I definitely needed them cleaned but could need some taken out, great that's all I need now, hope they leave me enough to eat with cus I love my food! I was given a few months berth from surgeries before my teeth were done so I was booked in for December and I'd be okay the next day so it wouldn't spoil my Christmas dinner! So in I went, mid-December and I knew I'd get something nice for tea and soft to eat. Luckily when mummy and daddy came to pick me up I was in a good mood! I didn't need any teeth out, I just needed a good clean and boy was I hungry, I was told I had tinned salmon for tea, I did think to myself I'd be happy to go in for surgery again if I got tinned salmon. I was told I was spoiled but after everything I've been through, I think it was well deserved and I think next time I'd like to try fresh salmon thank you very much as the tinned was lovely so how scrummy would the fresh be? I recovered well from all my surgeries.

Later in the year my awful cough came back and nothing seemed to stop or help it so it was said I was going in for more tests and they were sedating me again so they could see what was going on inside me.

I was there all day again and the tests shown that from previous results my lungs and chest had got slightly worse. I can't really tell you what the problems are except I had cancer previous to this as all the long names are hard to understand but the main thing is I was alright. I also needed a heart scan but I needed to be conscious for this so luckily didn't need to go under again. The heart scan went amazing, I didn't feel a thing, I fell asleep while they did it really, I did!! I was snoring like a tractor and all the staff were laughing at me and coming to listen to me. When they told mummy and daddy they laughed too and it became a joke that I could fall asleep anywhere. Imagine, being kept awake for a scan and ruddy well falling asleep, only I could do that. Oh Princess.

The scan did show that my heart had got slightly worse too but it wasn't of any concern, I've a leaky valve that sometimes makes me cough. I'm on medication for life now to help my heart and lungs and for pain relief for arthritis in my legs and spine.

Since I had these tests, we've been told its likely my cancer has come back too but it's been decided I'm having no more tests done or no more sedations as I'm an elderly lady now [a Princess now] and it's not good for me.

So I'm going to live the best life I can now and stay happy and as healthy as I can on my medication and have all the treatment I can.

That along with all the love and attention I get, I think I'll be ok. Oh and food, I do like my food so as long as I get fed I'll do just fine. Did I tell you that I have to take my medication in meat? Well, sometimes, I "accidently" drop the tablet when I eat the meat, it's

not a cheeky ploy to get more meat, really it isn't ......
The way I look at it is this, if they feeding me boiled
ham, or cooked chicken, I'm not going to refuse am I?
And if they wrap my medication in it it's not my fault if
they don't wrap it properly is it? If the tablet falls out,
well then try, try, try again. That's my method anyway.
I do love my food.

CHAPTER 8

TEAM TEDDY AND CO

I was introduced to Team Teddy the first day I came home. Mummy told me Teddy was really popular and had a massive worldwide following [she told me all about my sister Roxy too] I wondered if I could join in the group and if people would be kind enough to take me to their hearts and love me too. Mummy introduced me by showing my photo when I was a sorry looking little thing and said they were fostering me till after my surgeries. The messages and comments started straight away, people saying that my family wouldn't let me go and they'd adopt me etc etc. Mummy was adamant, no I'm definitely on foster and will be going back to be adopted by someone else. Did she have to eat her words a few weeks later when I was made a permanent member of the family and she told everyone I was officially adopted? Oh yes she did. They got called failed fosterers but wasn't that music to my ears? Oh yes it was.

Team Teddy [now called Team TeddyRoxyRuby] were all really supportive and instantly loved me, I got sent presents and treats and felt really accepted and loved. I had massive paws to step in to with Teddy being so loved, he really was the star of the internet and I did feel a bit worried how I'd follow him. But then mummy said that we are both totally different dogs with different backgrounds and different personalities and not to compare myself to Ted. We were both beautiful, we were both loved and we were both accepted by Team Teddy.

A few people did leave the group after losing Teddy, but more joined too and they knew I was here now so I like to think they joined cos of me as well as wanting to still follow Ted's page.

All in all I've been very supported by the team and I wanted to try to entertain them like Teddy did, I've accepted I'll never be as funny but I can be entertaining and do daily themes like he did to help people through their day too. It's lovely to think you can help someone who's sad, I know what it's like to be sad so if I can help one person then that makes me happy. I post photos of my beautiful self too which people love to see cus, well I'm a Princess now. Mummy films me at Christmas too like she did with Ted opening my advent calendar every day and they all like my spins, the more excited I get the more I spin and sometimes when I take my treats, I get mummy's finger too! I have 3 advent calendars and mummy always shows me the date on them to see if I can find it, I just think I want her to get on with it so I can get my belly filled but she does fuss around with them. I know it's all for entertainment but the quicker the better for me, I do like my food!

We have thousands of followers on the page and they are a lovely group of people. I get messages thanking me for cheering someone up, or I get asked for advice, and me being a clever girl, I get to help people out of their problems. We did think a few times about closing the page down but we know some people do rely on it and look forward to the daily themes we do. On a Monday we have "Mondays moans" where you can rant away and tell us what is on your mind and what is annoying you. Tuesday, we have "Tuesday's truths" where we tell you 3 truths and one lie and you have to guess what the lie is, it's only silly things and abit of fun, most people enjoy it. Wednesdays moans always go down well, it's me being Agony Aunt Ruby solving all your problems, again it's abit of fun so we don't ask for serious problems as you'll get a sarcastic answer. We then started doing "Wacky Wednesday", where we did silly things like an A-Z of animals, or stuff like we'd start a sentence and you had to finish it. Lot's of people joined in and it was fun. We have Thursday's theme" which is exactly as it says, a theme. So one week we might do "pretty girls" where you follow up by putting on a photo of your female pet, the next week would be "handsome male". So basically whatever theme it is it's a way to show off your pets and join in with abit of fun. Friday is "Ruby's riddles" where we put pictures on of things like food and you have to say if you like it or not, or it could be a "do you prefer" where you have choice of a few things to pick your favourite one. We also have a strange animal for you to guess what it is, it's a fun day and a lot join in and take part and I always get thanked for entertaining the group. Saturday's we sometimes have "Ruby's rib ticklers" where we tell jokes but we don't always do this due to lack of jokes. Finally, Sunday is "Rubys request" where I ask a question of the day and you tell me something related to the question, it's a popular quiz this one and helps to pass peoples days. The request could be something silly like "you have to give me the item on your right hand side, what do I get" and some answers are really funny. I'll get someone's husband or I'll get their medication, we do laugh. Another week it could be "have you any allergies" or an embarrassing one like, " tell me your most embarrassing moment". We had answers like having knickers caught in skirt or dress, having toilet roll stuck to your shoe, even had someone fall in a shop and pull a tablecloth off that had lots of plates and dishes on it that fell to the floor and smashed! [You know who you are hahaha]. So we tried to keep it fun for you all, even when we weren't feeling our best too, because this group is for you, Team TeddyRoxyRuby.

We'll keep the group open as long as you need us.

CHAPTER 9

HOLIBOBS n OUTINGS ... [Part one]

I've been on lots of holidays since I've had my forever home and I've loved each one. I had my first big proper day out only weeks after moving in when I went to Bakewell for the Carnival. It was two days before my first surgery so I wanted to enjoy myself and see what it's like being on days out. Storm was taking part in the Carnival, really she was, her dance school were doing a cheerleading routine and she was the team captain. We had ages to wait when we got there before they started the Carnival, we had to get there early as the roads were to be blocked off for safety. Storm had to stay with the dance school but me, mummy and daddy were free to do what we wanted. We went for a walk round the park first and I could see people looking at me, they were looking at my lumps and bumps which were coming off on Monday. I wasn't bothered as I knew I was loved now, mummy and daddy did tell some people what had happened to me but only cus they come to stroke me [they said I was beautiful not a sorry looking little thing] but all of them said I was very lucky, mummy said they were the lucky ones being able to adopt me.

We were all hungry, Storm was on a break from rehearsals but wasn't allowed to leave the park so me, mummy and daddy made our way to the chippy for dinner. I didn't know at this time what a chippy was but I soon got the smell of it once we were close by. My nose was going like the clappers and so was my tail. Mummy went inside to order the food and after a while she came out with a carrier bag and it smelled delicious. I kept trying to stick my nose in the bag for a better smell and was hoping there was something wrapped up in there for me. I was doing a dance all the way back to the park, walking and spinning and being all excited, I'm surprised they didn't have me join in with the Carnival with the moves I was throwing out there. We got back to where the people were waiting for the Carnival to start and gave Storm her dinner, now where's mine? Mummy pulled 3 wrapped up meals out of the bag and I knew there was one for me, first bag, chips and fish for daddy, second bag, chip butty with mushy peas for mummy, third bag? Two large succulent lovely smelling sausages for me! The only problem was they were hot and I had to wait for them to cool down, I don't like waiting for food, I love my food! After what seemed like a week and a half, the sausages had cooled down enough for me to eat them so daddy broke them up and put them down on a tray for me. They didn't last that long they were yummy. Now what are mummy and daddy going to give me? I did get a few chips and a bit of fish but I could have done another round of sausages! Never in a world of Princess's did I expect a sausage chippy dinner!

The Carnival started and we went in to one of the pubs to see the landlady who mummy and daddy knew as they stayed there a lot, apparently, she didn't know the sad news about Ted and hadn't met me so we went to say hello. The lady at first thought I was Ted [that happened a lot when I first got adopted] but then she realised I wasn't him and asked what happened. She was so upset when she heard he passed away but she was happy to meet me and to know I was now safe. They had a drink, Storm was driving so daddy could have a mucky beer, there wasn't any sausages though so I wasn't very impressed.

After the Carnival there was a dance display in the field and I loved it as there was a chip van nearby and everyone was eating chips so when I was smelling them, they asked if I could have one so I got lots of people feeding me chips! I had a lovely day for my first day out and we had a few overnight stays at Bakewell too.

The first time we stayed at Bakewell we stayed two nights, it was brilliant, sausage again at the chip shop and half of daddy's breakfast though I'm sure daddy did want some too! We did lots of things that weekend, we went round the park for walks, we went round the shops, we went to the pubs, we went to the pet shop for treats for me, though mummy had to pay out a few times as I saw some lovely treats and ate some out of the box [if it's good enough for Teddy it's good enough for me]. Then I picked a lovely big juicy treat all for myself to eat in the mucky pub while they had a drink. I had a lovely time those two days and ate far more than I should have but I didn't care, I was happy and if they offer me food I'm not going to say no am I? I do love my food.

We were back in Bakewell a few days later and staying for one night this time, I wondered why when we had only just come back but I wasn't complaining as they were happy to take me again as I'd been a really good girl. This time we were meeting mummy and daddy's friends who had met Teddy and now want to meet me. We were going for dinner in a pub so I hoped daddy got something meaty so I could share it. We met Tina, Mark and their dog Beau at the pub and they all hugged then made a fuss of me. I could smell the food and kept staring at the people serving it, I wonder if they'll trip and drop a plate? I could always help them clear it up.

Our food arrived and like I thought, daddy had meat, a pie, and I could smell the meat in it, I could see daddy putting chunks of it on the side of his plate and I knew they'd be for me once they had cooled down. Mummy gave me a few chips; she had some veggie sort of food but I didn't mind being fed off her plate too. I did have the meat off daddy's plate, it was lovely but I wasn't allowed to lick the plate afterwards like I do at home. [The plates wash so I can't see the problem].

After dinner we went to the cheese and wine shop and Tina bought a few different cheeses. I'm surprised mummy didn't buy any wine as she likes that as much as I love my food. After the cheese shop, Tina and Mark were leaving so we all said goodbye and I had pictures taken with Tina and Beau and we had some with mummy too. I was expecting to go home too but that's when I realised we were staying the night again really we were! Could I get a sausage from the chippy?

We went for a walk round the park first as it was getting dark and they wanted me to have a walk before the dark set in. That way they could do more mucky pubs and not have to worry about walking me again. I had to say I was shattered so I was happy when we got settled in the pubs and I could have a lie down and dream of the sausage I thought I wouldn't get. As we left one pub, we passed the chip shop and I stood still and looked at mummy, daddy was trying to get me to walk but I was rooted to the spot. Mummy realised I wanted feeding so said she would go and get me a sausage [at last] and boy did I enjoy it!

We met Tina and Mark again in Tamworth a few months later and it was a surprise to mummy. Tina had been messaging daddy asking to meet up but not to tell mummy so we could surprise her. They decided to meet at a pub halfway between where we each live so we could have dinner. Daddy told mummy we were off to look at a car for Storm as she was ready to take her driving test and needed a car. All this wasn't true, well Storm did need a car but we weren't off to look for one, it was a ploy to throw mummy off scent and she never suspected a thing. We set off to Tamworth and when daddy saw the pub we were meeting in, he made out that we were lost and asked mummy if she wanted to go for a drink while they sorted out the right route. Mummy said just to put the sat nav on for directions but daddy was adamant we were going in the pub. We went inside and mummy was stood at the bar, daddy told her to turn round and there sat behind her was Tina and Mark. Mummy turned round and then turned back to the bar before doing a double take and seeing Tina again! Mummy was all flummoxed and as she and Tina were hugging, even then mummy thought it was a coincidence and not a set up! Once all was explained we sat down for a chat and to order dinner, great, I'm starving! It was nice to see Beau again too. He settled down under the table but I was too busy watching the people bringing food again and wondering what I was having, I mean what daddy was having / sharing with me.

It had been a lovely afternoon and we had a laugh at mummy's face and reaction when she first saw Tina and Mark, we said we would meet up there again this year as it's not too far a drive for either of us but this time we're going to include mummy in the plans, hehehe.

We also met Tina and Mark at Bakewell again for Tina's birthday and this time we met Otis as well as Beau, he was only 9 months old when we met him and really bouncy and jumpy, he was lovely as is Beau. The family had previously met Bailey, their other dog who they sadly lost the year before. I was told that Teddy and Bailey got on really well and liked each other, it was sad to know they passed within only 7 months of each other.

BLACKPOOL … Staying with Julie and Steve. October 2022

The first time I went to Blackpool was the first time they went after losing Ted, really it was, and it was obviously hard for them all but mummy said it's something she had to do and face. What was special though is it was my 11th birthday while we there so it was hopefully going to make it better. It was October so we were hoping the weather was going to be dry at least so we could get out and we had a few meet ups to do too. On the drive down, mummy was saying she would find it strange going to back to where we lost Ted and she was crying most of the way down but she kept looking at me being all cute and excited on the back seat and I made her feel better. I was excited as even though I had some overnight stays at Bakewell I'd never been on holiday before so I was going on my first proper holibobs. I was going to see the beach and I was going on a tram as well; I know I'll get some lovely food and maybe a breakfast in the hotel too, I do love my food.

We arrived in Blackpool quite early and we couldn't check into the hotel until 3pm so we decided to find somewhere to park up and have a walk round. As we drove past the hotel, we saw Steve through the window and he waved at us so we stopped and parked outside the hotel. I was so excited, really I was, so this is Blackpool and this is where I'm staying. Steve said the room wasn't ready yet but we could leave the car and come in to say hello. He brought Julie down from upstairs as she was cleaning the room and they made the biggest fuss of me, well I don't think they've seen a Princess before and they certainly not had one stay with them. We had a lovely chat with them and said we'd see them later. We went for a walk and to get some dinner, good cus I'm hungry and I can smell seaside food. We had a meet up planned later so we were going to eat first then go to meet our friends, we haven't met them before but mummy talks to Sharon a lot on messenger. Anyway, food!!!! We walked past so many chippies and I was thinking "in all the world of Princess's why aren't we eating?" I can smell those sausages, I can practically taste those sausages, now get me those sausages!! Apparently, they always go to the same chippy cus they know it's nice it's just unfortunate it's the furthest one away!

Oh well, the further I walk the hungrier I get so hopefully I can have two sausages now. We finally get to the chippy and my belly thinks my throats been cut, I'm really starving. Mummy and Storm go into the chippy while me and daddy sit outside while they order the dinner. I see them come out of the chippy, not hard really being as I've not taken my eyes off the door since they went through it. The food smells just lovely, chips and beans, that's Storms, chips fish and peas, that's daddy's, chip butty with mushy peas on it, that's mummy's. I look at them all, I look the bag the food was in, where's mine? Just as I was about to start sulking, I saw another bag and guess what was inside it? Two sausages, not one, but two! They were jumbo ones as well, mummy said that if she knew they were that big she would have just bought me one, hehehe, well it's a good job she didn't know then but I'm sure I'll eat them, don't worry they won't go to waste. They didn't last long anyway let's say that!

After we had eaten, mummy rang Sharon to say we were in Blackpool as the arrangement they made was that we would hopefully be there for dinner time and mummy would let Sharon know so we could meet up. It turns out we were meeting in a pub, really, we were, I bet you don't believe me do you? I heard a conversation about "if you can't go in the pub on holiday then when can you?" It sounded good to me as I know I'd get lots of fuss, lots of treats and lots of rest. We arrived at the pub and met Sharon and her husband and I was a really good girl, I settled myself down until mummy went to the bar then I saw treats, there was a dog treat jar full to the top, it would be empty to the bottom once I'd finished with it, I tell-you. We had a really lovely few hours with them and they loved me, well of course they did I'm a Princess now, oh and the pub must have known I was coming as the carpet was red, fit for the entrance of a Princess.

As we left Sharon and her husband, we walked back to the hotel to check in and unpack. Daddy and Storm got the cases out of the car and brought them in while me and mummy went to the room to open up and for me to see the room for the first time. They had put us in room 3 where Teddy started being poorly but mummy was sort of glad as she said if she can face that she can face the rest of the holiday. We went in the room and you'll never what? I'd only got my own bag of treats all for me! I was looking round the room and wondering where to settle when Storm appeared with my bed, really, she did. I had my own bed brought over so that was me settled for the day, bed in the corner of the room and I'll be asleep in no time! What I didn't know was as soon as they had unpacked, we were off out again for a look round the shops [and probably to find another pub] so I was rudely disturbed. Just when I'd got myself comfy as well.

I dragged myself out of bed and we went down the stairs, me abit too quickly apparently as daddy wanted to walk down not run down, ooops sorry daddy. Well they've been telling me how nice it all is so I wanted to see it for myself. We had a walk on the side of the beach, I was allowed on as it was October so out of season but I didn't know what to make of it. I stepped on the sand and it felt funny, a nice funny, a different funny, a strange funny but I liked it. The sand on my little furry paws was one of the best feelings I've had, I was smiling, I was trotting, I was happy. I looked round and I could see they all had tears in their eyes they were so happy for me and I even did a little dance, I spinned round a few times then some of my feet left the ground like I was dancing and all I could hear behind me was "awwww look at her, awwww she's so happy, awwww I could cry for her" I didn't even mind them showing themselves up cus I was having the time of my life. We stayed on the sand until it was time to cross over the road to the shops and I was keeping my little furry paws crossed that we walked on the sand again on our back to the hotel.

We had a look around and mummy and Storm did some shopping, we walked past the chippy we had dinner in and I sat down hoping for more sausages, I got called a cheeky little madam and we carried on walking. We did walk up the beach again on the way back and I was having so much fun, mummy must have been having so much fun too as she almost forgot to get her camera out and take 96 photos that all look the same. I even had a pee pee on the sand really I did! I was having the time of my life and it was only the first day, if all the other days are as good as this, I'll be having a ball.

We went back to the hotel and this time I got my harness taken off which meant we were staying in for a while, we were going down to the bar later and if I wanted to, I could sleep down there, but then I'm nosey so I'll probably stay awake so I don't miss anything. Or any treats, I do love my food.

We went down to the bar about 8pm, which was when it opened for the night, apparently some guests had cancelled so there wasn't any other dogs there this week, oh well I can eat all the treats myself. There was a married couple there but they didn't have a dog, I took a liking to the lady [the man didn't go to the bar at night, just the lady] and I decided I wanted to sit with her. Mummy asked the lady if she was ok with me being at the side of her and she said yes, good job really as I wasn't moving, I was so comfy and I was tired so wanted to settle down. My ears did prick up though when I heard mummy order me a breakfast for the morning, with everything on it a dog was allowed! When I woke up, I was taken outside for a wee wee then I settled back down at the side of mummy and daddy for the rest of the time in the bar.

When we got up the next day I was taken back to the beach for a short walk and to do my business, it was only down the road from the hotel so it didn't take long to get there. I was so excited to be on the sand again and

I loved the sand as it was all cold and soft. I had a walk and mummy was there again with the phone [camera] snapping away taking my photo, I did a massive smile and it made mummy and daddy laugh. We were meeting Storm in the breakfast room as she didn't want to come out that morning but she did the rest of the week. We made our way back to the hotel and I was thinking about my breakfast, I thought I could eat mine then still have some of daddy's as well!

We went in for breakfast and Storm was waiting for us, it's the first time I've seen the breakfast room and I was really happy to see a note on the table "Ruby Trixie and family" it made me feel really special, I was the most important one. Mummy got me some dry food, I looked at her, does she really think I'm going to eat that dry stuff when I've a cooked breakfast coming? It wasn't long before Julie came out to take our order, she told me my breakfast was on its way and my mouth was watering. Out it came, my breakfast, all for me, bacon, sausage, scrambled egg, black pudding, and it didn't last long it was in my belly before you could say Ruby Trixie. Now, what's daddy having? I did sneak abit of daddy's breakfast too, I know you'll think that I had enough of my own but daddy will get fed later so he can spare some. The best thing about it is, when we'd finished, Julie came out with a sausage and some bacon that was left over, guess whose belly that went in? And no, it wasn't daddy's!

We needed to walk our breakfast off so out we went, we walked the other way this time and walked up the beach again until we had to cross the road. It happens that where we crossed the road was near the pub we went in yesterday, what's the odds we'll end up back in there again? I'll bet you a sausage that I'm right. I stayed outside the shops with daddy while mummy and Storm looked round, they seemed to be in the shops for ages and they always come out empty handed. At least buy something while you're leaving me.

They decided to get the tram into Fleetwood, mummy said it was hard going back cus that's where Teddy's last day was but she said again she needs to face it as long as we don't go on the beach, that would be too much. Before we came away mummy contacted Janet and Sheila with Dexter to see if they wanted to meet me but asked them to meet in Blackpool not Fleetwood as she can't face that beach. Unfortunately Sheila had plans that week and Janet was away but we decided to go anyway and do some shopping and have a look around. So we got on the tram, my very first time and I was a trooper, really I was. I sat at daddy's feet and enjoyed everyone looking at me and saying how beautiful I am, I know I'm beautiful but I do like hearing people tell me. It was quite a long ride to Fleetwood but I did have fun, my first time on the tram hopefully won't be my last.

We got off the tram and they were straight in the shops; I hope they buy something this time if I have to wait outside. To be honest I was just wondering where the nearest chippy was, or any food place really cus they did say they weren't having chips every day. I didn't mind what we had as long as I got fed, I do love my food. I also know I've had breakfast but I'm a growing girl and that was two hours ago. Mummy and Storm were in and out of shops and it must have been thirsty work because somehow we ended up in a pub, it were more like a social club and the best thing was its dog friendly. The main reason they went in or so they say is cus they all needed the toilet and couldn't find any public ones, so use the pub ones instead. We walked in and all I could hear was "awwww look at you aren't you beautiful" and everyone was staring at me, I thought about going back out the door and making a grand entrance this time. Now I know how Teddy felt, being told all the time how beautiful he was, now they're saying it about me too. A few people came over to stroke me and fuss me and I was lapping it all up, one man even gave me some treats, I think I'll go and sit at the side of him, hehehe. They got a drink after the loo visits and said it was so nice in there it would be a shame just to have one drink, well then, I definitely am going to sit with that man cus my family weren't feeding me!

We ate at the pub that night, I say we, I got scraps off daddy's plate while they all had plate fulls, but I knew I'd get some food when we got back to the hotel. I went on another tram too, well I had to really as we had to get the tram back to Blackpool, I fell asleep on the way back, all that looking for food and not being fed made me sleepy. We went back in the bar that night too and I spent most of the night on the settee sleeping in between mummy and daddy, luckily I got fed before we went to the bar, I do like my food.

The Tuesday was my birthday, I was 11 [we think], as I said earlier there were no other dogs there that week to help me celebrate but I did have a great birthday, the first one in all my years that I celebrated. Mummy bought some doggy cupcakes and gave one to Julie to give their dog Barney. I had an extra breakfast that day too and Julie gave me some packs of treats for my birthday. We walked to Stanley Park that day, we didn't know our way there so Storm put the sat nav on her phone. Apparently, they were going to take Ted the day they lost him so thought they'd make it special and take me on my important day. It was quite a long walk but we kept stopping for a rest, it was a warm day for October and I heard something about an ice cream in the park so I was overly excited. We made it to the park and had a walk round, mummy found a feather as soon as we arrived, hello Teddy.

We spent a while there and finally found the ice cream place, mummy was talking to the lady who was serving and I was getting restless, didn't she know the quicker she shut up and ordered the quicker I get my lips round some food. When they eventually got served, I was offered some of mummy's ice cream off her finger, it was nice too, and mummy's finger cus I bit it before I realised I was supposed to lick. I did get some more too but I was told I can't have a lot as it could give me belly ache, I thought back to when I lived on the streets and the crap I ate then so I don't think a few licks of ice cream will hurt me. I did get spoiled though that day I got more treats than I should have had and I did have the extra breakfast.

When we got back to the hotel, we opened my cards and presents as mummy brought them with her, I was so popular! I was so happy! I was really tired cus my little paws opened so many things! I had money, I had treats, I had lots and lots of presents and I had lots of people who loved me, thanks Team TeddyRoxyRuby. I couldn't have too many of my treats though as mummy said again that I'd get a poorly belly. I did however get some chicken for my tea that mummy sneaked into the shop for and gave me when we got back to the hotel and I can tell you it was yummy.

We did a few more meet ups this holiday, we met Joan and she brought me some lovely sausages that didn't last long, we met her near the wall that Teddy jumped over, I hope they don't think I'm going to do that! After meeting Joan we went to meet Sue with her son [who drives her down to meet us] and their dog also called Ruby. We met at the Solarias and had a drink and a chat, oh and I was given treats, it seemed rude not to eat them. I didn't fall asleep as I was too nosey, lots going off and people ordering food, lovely smelling food that I was hoping someone would drop so I could snatch it. On a different day we met up with Jane and Simon in the pub we went to the previous Sunday. I was a superstar really I was, not only did Jane fall in love with me, I was getting lots of attention from other people in there too. I just hoped mummy remembered when she went to the bar that the treat jar was at side of it. We had a few drinks in the pub then went for a walk with Jane and Simon so they could see me on the beach and see what a good and clever girl I am. We said goodbye as we got close to our hotel and we went back for a rest till it was time to go to the bar.

I had a fantastic first holibobs, really I did, I had a breakfast each morning, I had sausages when they had chippy, I had food off daddy's plate when we went to the pubs to eat and I had lots of treats. I also had chicken when mummy bought me some from the shop so I didn't get fed up of dog food. I ate my dog food but if they want to get me something nice and treat me then I'm not going to say no am I? Not only did I have a fantastic holibobs I had a great birthday too and certainly felt like the Princess I am.

Tattershall … [Storm's 18th]

My second proper holibobs was February 2023 and we were going to Tattershall Lakes for Storm's 18th birthday and staying in a lodge. Tattershall used to be mummy's happy place but since we lost Ted she still loves going but won't call it the happy place now. Also she won't stay in any of the accommodation they stayed in with Ted as they were happy memories. They're making new happy memories with me now. We set off the first day of our holibobs and the car was jam packed full, I was taking two beds, yes two, my living room and my bedroom bed so no matter where I was sleeping, I had my own bed. Then we were taking our own food, and beer, and beer, oh we were taking our own beer too did I say that? Before Tattershall we were calling at Woodhall Spa, a place they always went first as we can't check into the lodge until 3 o'clock, so rather than lose a day of the holiday we're calling at Woodhall Spa first.

We found somewhere to park up then walked straight into what looked like the woods we go in at home, I loved it, different smells and lots of grass and mud to walk on. I was having fun and didn't want to leave but then I heard them saying about going for a sandwich and my ears pricked up. I practically ran out of the woods then to get to the shop; I do love my food. Mummy and Storm went in the shop and I was stood outside admiring all the food in the window it all looked so tasty. I was hoping they'd bring something out for me. Mummy came out carrying a massive bag and before I was allowed to see what was in it, they decided to find somewhere to sit down so we could eat without dropping anything. I don't know what they were bothered about cus I'd soon hoover it up. They found a seat and I'm spinning round in excitement to see what I've got. Ham salad for daddy, cheese salad for mummy, quiche for Storm and 3 massive cut off the bone slices of ham for me!

It's not far from Woodhall to Tattershall so just before 3pm we set off to check in to our lodge and it wasn't long before we were there and I have to say it was beautiful, such a lovely view and lots of grass to play on. After we had got the key and we were driving to our lodge, I saw lots of ducks and geese just walking round on the grass, crossing the road, they didn't care they were holding us up cus we had to wait for them, never even bothered that a Princess was awaiting her lodge. After driving round for what seemed like a day, we finally found the lodge after going the wrong way so many times and it was lovely, never in a world of Princess's did I think it would be so nice. I think I'll like it here, my home for the week. We unpacked, well I say we, I waited until my living room bed was put down then jumped straight in it, this holibobs lark is tiring. I just watched them bring everything in then we had a look round the lodge. It was beautiful, the living room was massive then we had decking outside with a hot tub, I wonder how many hours mummy and Storm will spend in that. They had a massive storage room too that could have fitted a bed in, mummy said if daddy snores or gets on her nerves he can sleep in there hehehe! My other bed got put in the bedroom so I knew I'd be ok.

For the first night they decided to go to the club house, just as I thought I could get settled and rest. It was a longish walk as we were right round the other side but they knew a short cut and said by the time we get there they be ready for a drink. I thought, by the time we get there I be ready for bed. The thing is I could fall asleep and rest down there but you see, I'm so nosey I like to see what's going on and I don't like to miss out on anything. And my nose will be going like the clappers when the food orders come out and if anyone drops anything I need to be there to hoover it up, I do like my food.

They had a few drinks and I was getting my bearings, I like to know where things are, I've seen the entrance now to the kitchen so I know where that is, and I know what uniform the staff wear so I can stalk them for food.

We walked back to the lodge later on and I was looking forward to a sleep, my little legs had worked overtime today. I knew when we were back that mummy and daddy would be watching the telly for a while so I could get my sleep. It was fun as when they relaxed with the telly on, the bedroom door was left open so I could either go in my bed in the lounge or my bedroom one, choices choices. I did stay in the lounge with mummy and daddy until they went to bed then I got in my nighttime bed and slept til the morning. It's funny cus I never heard them get up and never heard them talking but what I did hear was the breakfast been made, ok it was only toast but I do always have the corners or the crusts off the toast so I thought I'd best get up. I walked in the lounge and daddy said "hello buggerlugs have you finally woke up?" It's funny what the smell of toast does. I went outside first for a wee wee then sat at side of mummy and daddy while they had my toast, I mean their toast, haha, no I do mean my toast being as I had more than them.

That holibobs we went all over really we did, we had no set plans except to go to Mablethorpe on Thursday as that was Storms birthday and it's what she chose to do as she loves it there. So in the week we went to Skegness which was so windy we had to hide in the shops, really we did. We only just stepped on the beach and nearly got swept in the sea it was windier than I've ever known it. We decided to go for a walk and maybe try the beach later if the wind died down. Storm and mummy went round the shops and me and daddy waited outside, it wasn't as windy away from the beach, well until I let one off hahaha. I had lots of people coming up to me outside the shops saying how beautiful I am and asking to stroke me, I do love a fuss, nearly as much as I love my food! Talking of food, when are we eating?

One morning we went down to the club for breakfast, I was hoping daddy would have his usual full English then he'd share it with me. While looking at the menu they saw that they had "mega massive full breakfast" it was 3 times the size of a normal full English, great that's me fed, now what's daddy having? Hahaha. We did order it and me and daddy shared it, he said when he orders a normal sized breakfast, he hardly gets any so if he orders a massive one he would get his share and I can have more than usual. Mummy ordered a veggie breakfast [no egg] and Storm had American pancakes with fruit. I've got to tell you though, that breakfast was just the best, I didn't get just bits of bacon, sausage and black pudding, I got whole ones! And hash browns too! Daddy did struggle to eat what he had so he was pleased I was there to help him with it. Now, what's mummy giving me? I do love my food.

We went to Horncastle as well during the week, it's got lots of charity shops and it's something that mummy and Storm love, a charity bargain. It was a nice place with a nice chip shop, they did lovely sausages, I had two really I did! We went on a walk too near a park and it was nice but my little legs were getting tired. It was decided to go back to the lodge early and mummy and Storm could use the hot tub. It had been a lovely day but I'd had enough so while they were in the hot tub I was laid on my bed but I kept my eye on mummy til I fell asleep.

So, let's talk about Mablethorpe and Storm's birthday. She opened some of her presents and cards the night before as she had so many then opened the rest the next day, she had been given lots of money so she was looking forward to spending it. We drove to Mablethorpe and parked up down the road from the beach. We were meeting Liz at the coffee shop first for a drink and she hasn't met me before but she had met Teddy a few times and loved him. Of course she was going to love me too, I'm like a Princess now, and she did! I liked Liz too and was more than happy when she bought me two sausages! We spent time with Liz then walked up to the beach to meet Carol who they've also met before. Carol had 3 little cute dogs who were playing on the beach, I had a little play but it was all new to me but I did enjoy myself and the dogs were friendly.

Storm chose to go to the pub for dinner, dog friendly and sells food, good choice. She could also have her first legal drink because today she was 18. She had her driving licence ready to show ID and we did laugh as when she went to the bar and ordered the drinks she wasn't asked for proof of age! The man just served her really, he did, and we thought it was funny cus all she wanted all along was to be asked for proof of age. We had a lovely dinner, I say we as I had bits off each plate, well I am a Princess now! They all had sausage, mash and peas, mummy and Storm's was veggie but I'm not fussy, if it's food I'll eat it and that beach air made my belly hungry. After dinner we did some shopping and Storm spent some birthday money, she was coming out of shop after shop with bags and bags, she made me tired looking at her. She asked if we could go back to Tattershall and go to the pub next door, it belongs to Tattershall but it's a separate building. Storm said she fancied a cocktail; we'd been in the pub the day before and she had a non-alcoholic one so this time wanted a proper cocktail. Mummy told her not to have too many and to be careful as we were going to the club again tonight with it being her birthday and hopefully she could get asked for ID there, being as she wanted it so much.

We had some time in the lodge when we got back so they could all get showered and ready to go out, I was glad cus I slept for a few hours and was all refreshed for sniffing that food the people were serving. The walk down to the club that night didn't seem as long as last time, maybe cus I'd had a rest but it didn't seem to take as long to get there. As we walked into the bar we were asked if we were eating and if we needed a table, even though they had pub dinner they said they'd have some snacky bits, my ears pricked up cus I knew I'd get fed again. We were shown to a table then mummy and Storm went to get drinks, mummy was laughing when they came back as yet again Storm hadn't been asked for proof of age! She was more annoyed as we had been at Tattershall since Saturday and she been drinking soft drinks, if they not asked for ID tonight she said she may as well have had alcohol all week! Never mind the drink, where's the food?? A lady came to take the order and she saw Storm was wearing an "18" badge and said she would get her a free shot, is it time to order food yet? Finally, we have our food order, nachos for mummy and Storm [that's ok I can have some cheese] and chips for daddy [I love chips] and luckily the food came before the shot Storm was having so I didn't have to wait long. The hot tub got lots of use that week, me and daddy sat inside or on the decking if the night was quite warm. I loved it though when they came in as it meant that we were all snuggled up in the lounge, they had a drink and watched telly and I was all snug in my bed.

We had a lovely week and Storm had a lovely birthday, I was a really good girl and they were all proud of me too. I had lots of lovely food and was spoiled, I had lots of walks too, I really enjoyed myself but I was glad to be home and looking forward to my next holibobs. I'd been to different seaside places all in a few days and loved the sand on my paws. It's amazing how apart from the cheap shops that sell the same things, how different the places are. I do think my favourite place was Mablethorpe as everything is mainly close together and the beach is dog friendly all year round, at least the part we went on is. Never in a world of Princess's did I think I'd be so lucky to go to so many different places in a week.

We had takeaway the night we got home as after all the washing and cleaning mummy didn't want to cook. The kebab that daddy shared with me was lovely, especially reaching for it from his fingers that I nearly ate too. I had lots of the kebab meat then tried my luck for some pizza and cheesy chips, I don't mind what I have as I do like my food. I'm ready for bed now I'm absolutely shattered, really I am.

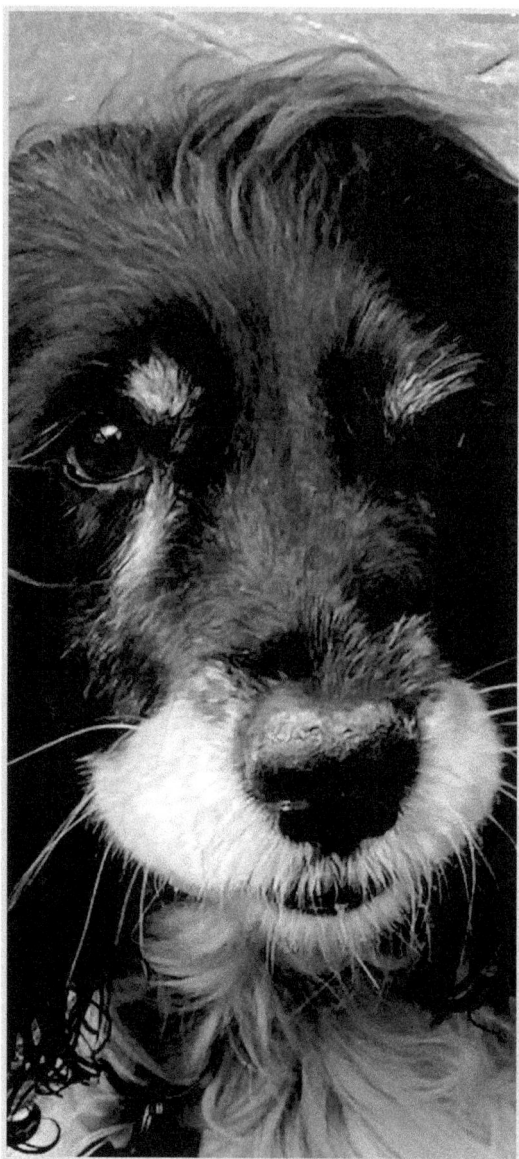

CHAPTER 10

HOLIBOBS n OUTINGS [Part two]

BLACKPOOL Part 2. August 2023

We had booked to go back to Blackpool in October but we didn't realise that Storm didn't get the same half term break at university like she did at school so we had to change the dates. Luckily Julie and Steve had availability to bring us forward to August when Storm was able to go. Reece again chose to stay home, since he's been old enough to stay home alone, he's chosen to do so, [mummy says she don't even want to know what he's up to, as long as the house is still standing, the cats are fed and alive and he looks after Teddy's Garden, she's happy]. So we were going at the beginning of August for a week and I was excited cus I knew what to expect. They said this time they were going to get a weekly tram pass so we could travel on that more and save my legs, they didn't want to tire me out with all the walking. We used the tram a lot, mainly down to a pub called The Gynn, it did really good food and Storm got a liking for it so we ate there a lot that week. We had a really lovely breakfast at the hotel and I got my own breakfast again too, then we ate at the pub for tea. We went to Cleveleys on the tram, and Fleetwood, also using it to go up past the Pleasure beach sometimes as it's quite a walk up to there. We did walk along the sea front a lot though and I had the sand in my paws. Each morning before breakfast we would walk along the seafront too for me to do my business and get some fresh air.

We checked in at the hotel and when we first got there, I made my way to the steps where the bar is, aren't I clever going to the bar first? I've been trained correctly! The bar wasn't open though yet so we made our way upstairs and unpacked our bags, well they did, I was too excited spinning round the room! I'd got some treats left me again and I wondered when mummy would let me have them. As we were unpacking, Julie knocked on the door and wanted mummy, well you're not going to believe this in all the world of Princess's, you really won't. Julie gave mummy a white feather and said in all the 30 years of owning the hotel this had never happened. Julie was cleaning the room that morning and on the floor was a white feather, this was the same room in which they lost Ted. So mummy had goosebumps, Julie had goosebumps and they were both close to tears, how uncanny. Mummy thanked Julie and kept the feather somewhere safe, well hello Ted, you've just made mummy's holiday. She said if there's no more signs ever again that Ted is around, she don't mind cus he came through when she needed him and knowing he's here then he's given his approval for mummy to enjoy the holiday. Teddy your still so selfless.

We met up again with Sue and her son Mark and the beautiful Ruby and also with Jane and Simon [on different days] we didn't meet Joan this time as she wasn't too well. It was nice to see them all again, we met them in the usual places, it's mainly because we can sit inside so if it rains, we are okay. We went to the pub we meet Jane and Simon at for tea a few times too, as well as the Gynn. I don't know why we can't just eat at the chippy it's a lot easier for me to have my own sausages than to have to wait to be fed off someone's plate.

This time there were other dogs in the hotel so we saw each other at night in the bar and in the breakfast room, we all got on ok but we didn't play a lot. There was another Ruby there too, a little Yorkie girl and she was from Sheffield, we made friends with her mummy Sam and keep in touch. I spent most of the nights in the bar sleeping, but I did play a tiny bit with other dogs before I slept. I only woke up when I heard the treat bags opening and went to sit with whoever had them so I got my share, then I went back to sleep.

We did lots of shopping again but not as much walking with having tram tickets, I got lots of fuss on the trams, people were staring at me and smiling at me, I did a head tilt looking at them then they "awwwwed" at me. I was really good on the trams and sat at daddy's feet, one day though I could smell chips in someone's bag and daddy had to hold my lead tight or I would have been off to sit with them. One of the trams was really busy and we had to squeeze on, we would have waited for the next one but we'd been waiting ages so got on it. Mummy had her walking stick and someone generously gave their seat up for mummy to sit down, I wondered when I'd get a seat, being a Princess now. On one of the trams, the conductor was fussing me and stating the obvious, telling me I'm gorgeous, and when we got the tram back the same day it was the same conductor, really it was! Think he's been waiting for me hahaha.

On the last day of the holibobs though I was shattered, even though we got trams we did do a lot of walking especially in the mornings, we had a really good walk on the seafront before breakfast like I've told you. The last morning of our stay, we said that after breakfast we were going to drive to the top end of the beach where dogs can go on but that didn't happen. We went for what was supposed to be my last seafront pee pee and walk [before breakfast] and I just thought to myself that I wasn't going, I did my pee pee as we walked out of the hotel then turned round and walked back. Mummy and daddy chuckled at me and asked me, "are you too tired Rube" and I just looked at them and walked back into the hotel. I wasn't too tired to eat my breakfast though and look what everyone else was having. I had my usual breakfast but I'm going to shock you now….. I didn't eat it all! Everyone was shocked and mummy said they'd finally managed to fill me up. I laid down and waited for everyone to finish eating their breakfast, then guess what? I got up and ended up eating the rest of my food! They did all chuckle at me being a Princess, well did you really expect me to leave it? I do like my food!

We didn't go to the beach, I was too tired so we drove to a shop Storm wanted to spend her last bit of money in. She had seen something a few days before and said if she had any money left at the end of the holiday she would go back for it. After that we drove home. I slept all the way home in the car, and all night in my bed. I slept all day Saturday, only getting up to do my business and have my food and the same the most of Sunday. I was on the settee mostly and was so comfy I didn't even move when mummy sat at the side of me though I did like the ear rubs and belly rubs she gave me. I was ready for a walk on Monday when I'd rested my little paws all weekend though we didn't go far. I was disappointed though after having my morning walks at Blackpool then having my lovely doggie fry up breakfast, when I got back from my walks at home I was greeted with dog food, really, dog food!

We unfortunately cancelled our next visit to Blackpool that would have been the end of July 2024. My legs aren't as good as they were and my family are concerned that it would be too much for me, going up and down stairs in the hotel. Also with Blackpool being as busy as it is, it could prove too much for me, even though I now have a Princess carriage [more of that later.]

My family obviously want to do what's best for me and make my remaining time as easy and relaxing for me as possible. I've had two lovely holibobs there so I don't really mind.

As we cancelled the holibobs, the hotel also announced they were closing for a while, Julie and Steve's dad is unwell and they obviously need to care for him and put him first. So at the time of writing this, it's closed til further notice and we wish the lovely family all the best and we send them lots of love.

If anyone wants the name of this wonderful hotel we stay at it's called THE CHESTERFIELD PET FRIENDLY B&B and it's on Wellington Road, Blackpool. It's worth going it's a beautiful place. Lovely home cooked breakfast, with dog shaped fried bread, and a varied menu, they cater for veggies, vegans, and they do kippers, crumpets and a variety of food. There's also cereal, fruit and yoghurts for you to help yourself. There's a dog table where they have dried food and dishes for water it's a lovely set up. The bar is open from 8pm and Julie and Steve can't do enough for you. We wouldn't stay anywhere else now. With or without a dog, it's definitely worth a stay.

EYAM ... A day out

We met up with Sheila, Billy and their dog Kopper for a day out, mummy and daddy have met Sheila before in Norfolk but she's not met me, she met Ted that day. We've not met Billy or Kopper before and we were all looking forward to a nice day. The weather didn't start off nice, it was raining and miserable but we said we were still going to meet up. We were meeting in a car park in Eyam and taking the day as it came or playing it by ear as mummy said. When we first saw them, we went over for hugs and I got lots of fuss, mummy and daddy fussed Kopper, he was really handsome, [blushes].

Sheila had made mummy a beautiful ornament of Ted and they had another hug and a few tears.

We set off to go for a walk, it was only a small village type place but it was lovely. As we were walking round, we saw a café and decided to go for a hot drink as it was raining again. We sat outside under a sort of hut which was really cosy and lovely. Sheila and mummy were talking and so were daddy and Billy, I was under the table with Kopper, no not like that!!! I'm a lady [like a Princess now] and I'm sure Kopper is a gentleman too. What we were really doing under the table was sheltering from the rain and relaxing cuz we knew we would be off walking again soon. When they had finished their drinks, it had about stopped raining and we set off for another walk, we ended up near a Church which mummy and Sheila went in for a look around and took some photo's.

There's alot of history at Eyam and there was plaques scattered around with information on them for visitors to read, which the adults did. Me and Kopper were sniffing round, that's how we got our information of what was going off!

As it was getting abit later we ended up having a drink in a pub, it got my interest as we sat near the kitchen entrance so whenever a food order came out, the staff had to walk past me. They were all laughing at me as I was determined I was going to get some, my nose was sniffing and twitching and my eyes didn't leave the door, well till someone walked past me then my eyes didn't leave them! I was wondering if to stick out a paw or two in the hope that someone would trip over but daddy had a tight hold of me so I couldn't go far, I think he knew my way of thinking! It's not my fault at all, I just love my food! Anyway if they had brought me some food of my own, I wouldn't be wanting food from others would I? [yes I would hehehe]. After a drink and lots of chats we made our way back to the car park ready to go home. It had been a lovely day and it was nice to meet them all, mummy and Sheila were happy to see each other again and it was nice to meet Billy and to see Kopper, especially when we behaved under that table.

CHAPTER 11

THE FIRST TIME I ...

The first time I started to run on the field, mummy was really over the moon and was nearly crying saying what a big girl I was and stood clapping at me. I was so happy and pleased with myself that I did it again to show her how clever I was. She was all excited and giddy so she just had to tell my daddy.

The first time I licked my little paws and washed my ears apparently was so cute. Mummy saw what I was doing and she looked at me and coooed and said I was so beautiful and she loved my little paws. I did it again and got the same reaction, mummy was saying it melted her heart and was so excited and giddy she just had to tell my daddy.

The first time I ran upstairs and tried to escape having my outdoors coat put on to go for a walk was ultra cute and funny [apparently], I saw the coat and decided I didn't want to wear it so took myself upstairs. Mummy was laughing and said I was cheeky but I still didn't come down. Eventually I was coaxed down by some treats, mummy was so excited and giddy she just had to tell my daddy.

The first time mummy spoke to Storm on facetime I could hear Storm but couldn't see her. I was looking round to see where she was so mummy turned the phone so Storm could see me. It took a while for me to realise what was happening then out of the blue, I did a booper to the phone [put my nose on the screen], well you should have heard them both! They were both saying " awwww Rubes your so cute" and saying it was of the sweetest things I've ever done. Mummy was so excited and giddy she just had to tell my daddy.

The first time I gave paw, I didn't actually give paw…. Mummy thought I gave paw but I actually thought she had something for me and I was going to feed me [I do love my food] so I was actually starting to do my spins, but mummy thought I was giving paw. She held my paw and shook it as though she was saying hello, I mean I don't want to upset her and tell the truth as she was all excited and giddy, she just had to tell my daddy.

The first time I went on the back garden on my own accord was again apparently so cute. I decided to go and lay outside on my comfy blanket and get some sleep in the shade. I'm never outside on my own so mummy came out to sit with me, she saw me put my little head on my little paws and was all excited and giddy she just had to tell my daddy.

The first time I kissed mummy she was so happy she cried, I don't give kisses out very often so mummy was really privileged. She was all excited and giddy she just had to tell my daddy.

The first time I lifted my front paw up while laid in my bed was cus I wanted a tickle. I love underneath my paws been rubbed and felt in a cheeky mood. I was half asleep but saw mummy walk past me so I laid on my side and cheekily lifted up my paw, mummy tickled me and I had a smile on my face, she was so excited and giddy she just had to tell my daddy.

The first time I walked next door to Spikes house without a lead on, mummy was so proud of me, we had been looking after Spike all day and it was time for him to go home. Usually mummy takes me round with my harness and lead on but this time I was lead free. I walked down our steps then did a little trot to next door, almost breaking into a run! Mummy says I was so cute! I did run up the steps to Spikes house though as I was sure I'd get some treats off his daddy for being a good girl. [I did get a treat] When we got home, I could see mummy was proud of me, and she was all excited and giddy she just had to tell my daddy.

The first time I went to the pet shop and stole a treat, I made people laugh, lots of people saw me pinch it off the shelf and lay in the shop and eat it. No one said anything as it was so comical, even a member of staff saw it. They all just stood watching me and I even gave them a little smile afterwards! Mummy was so excited and giddy but didn't have to tell my daddy cus he saw it all and said I was a cheeky bugger!

CHAPTER 12

HOW LUCKY AM I?

I never thought I'd be so lucky not to only have a family that love me but to have other people to love me too. Everywhere I go I get attention from people, either wanting to stroke me or giving me treats. How lucky am I?

I'm never left alone. If my family go out, they always take me with them, even if their going shopping then I'll stay in the car with daddy while mummy goes in the shops. If for any reason they can't take me with them then I'll go next door to Spike and his daddy and they'll look after me. How lucky am I?

Once I had all my surgery stitches out and my scars had healed and fur had grown back, I had a personal fitting for a new coat and harness, really, I did. I was excited for the harness as it meant no more lead attached to my collar, but the coat, not so much. Anyway, mummy knows someone who runs a pet shop so she made an appointment for me to have fittings. I've got to tell you I quite fancied myself in that harness, I looked lovely and it was my very first one. I did parade myself around when I went out in it. I also got a coat that I wasn't bothered about but knew I had to have. I did feel special though having my own personal assistant to dress me. How lucky am I?

I've told you already that I've got 3 beds, well I'm allowed on the settee too, really, I am. Sometimes I love laying in my downstairs bed but other times I want to lay on the settee. I can't always make it up by myself though so mummy has to help me by pushing up on my bum. I've got it easy really if you think about it cus I put my two front paws on the settee, look at mummy then she hutches me up with no effort at all from me. How lucky am I?

In the mornings daddy usually gets up first. Mummy will usually stay in bed til she hears me get up and start spinning round the bedroom. I won't go downstairs without mummy so she comes downstairs with me while I go outside [for a tiddle] then she goes back upstairs to get dressed. So, I've got daddy giving me lots of fuss when I come back in the house and mummy giving me lots of fuss when she comes downstairs. How lucky am I?

Mummy went to town one day for an appointment and called in the market afterwards for a few bits. Some of the few bits she got were for me, really, they were. She called to get daddy some cockles and whelks, [daddy says I wouldn't like them but how does he know cus he's never let me try them, he's too tight to let me have one!] Anyway, once I saw what mummy had bought me, I didn't want daddy's silly seafood cus I got liver and heart really I did!!! While mummy was cooking it, she was pulling faces, she got blood dripping down her arm and she was doing a silly dance. I thought she was trying to join in with me and start spinning round, I nearly called mummy "Kylie" that time, [you don't want to imagine mummy in gold hot pants ....] When the liver and heart was cooked and cut up, I was told to wait til it cooled down, now it's definitely time to spin round it smells lovely! Come on mummy, lets spin and dance now! I've never had it before and I can tell you it was yummy in my tummy. Mummy says she hates cooking it cus she's a veggie and hates the look and smell of it so she must love me very very much. How lucky am I?

When mummy makes a donation to my rescue with money that we raised for charity we always take it to the charity shop. We usually go on a Monday when Heather is there who is a trustee and let my family adopt Ted and me. When we go, I'm always allowed to go into the shop and get a fuss, and a treat! We always hand over the money and any general donations to the shop like household stuff or clothes that we don't need now. They're always grateful, really, they are, and I'm grateful too as I get taken back to my rescue but then get taken back home after. How lucky am I?

I lay on the settee at night sometimes at the side of mummy and she always strokes me, after a while I get up, turn around and sit really close to mummy and she says "aww you coming for a snuggle Princess?" and she strokes my pretty face, my belly, my neck fur and my little paws. I love having my ears rubbed mostly really, I do. How lucky am I?

I don't like going to the vets but I do get lots of treats and fuss when I go. All the staff love me, the receptionists, the vets, the nurses, everyone! I get lots of fuss and they're always happy to see me. I think they have soft spot for me cus of my history and now they can see how beautiful I am and how happy I am. Oh, and how well fed I am! What I do like though, is, I always get treats, one lady will give me treats then when she's fed me, I'll get treats off someone else who hasn't seen I've already had some! Well I'm not going to tell them am I? No way am I missing out on treats! I love my food. How lucky am I?

I've been going to York a lot to see Storm at University, really, I have. She's staying in the student halls and when we go to see her, I always go in to her room, I shouldn't do and one time we did get told off for being inside [we had Spike that time too] a man came in to the halls and said dogs weren't allowed inside. I've been back in since, hehehe, they sneaked me in really, they did! I love it in there cus Storm's got a full length mirror and I do like to look at myself in it! I just stand and admire how beautiful I am until it's time to leave. I get taken into the kitchen after for a drink of water then I get smothered in kisses by Storm before we leave to come home. It's a lovely day out. How lucky am I?

Each time I have my medication it gets put in some meat, slices of ham or chicken, I'm not fussy which, I do like my food. The thing is I'll have my breakfast afterwards so I feel like I've been fed twice, really, I do. The same happens at teatime so I'll have my medication in the meat. I'm not complaining as I think it's the perfect set up, especially when the tablets drop out of the meat so I have to have another slice with the tablets wrapped in again! How lucky am I?

Daddy built a pergola outside so that we can sit out no matter what the weather, it's all sheltered off and really cosy. Mummy's got her egg chair she sits in, we've lots of seating around with blankets and cushions so it's all comfy when people come round or we sit outside. The best thing about it though is, I've got two beds out there now, really, I have! Two beds! They do laugh at me though as I'll lay in one of my beds then get up and lay on the decking. It's good as I have a choice where I want to lay and I can lay and watch the birds in the garden and the squirrel run across the fence. How lucky am I?

At night I'm always after food and don't always settle until I know I'm definitely not getting any, I know that when all the family are settled down. I do like to make a nuisance of myself though sometimes and go in and out of the kitchen til mummy follows me. Most of the time I'll get a treat and it's usually my licky mat with liver paste on, it's my favourite and keeps me quiet for all of ten minutes when I've got it. I get in all the nooks and crannies and lick all the liver paste, so it pays to be a nuisance sometimes. How lucky am I?

CHAPTER 13

CHRISTMAS 2022 n 2023

I didn't really know what Christmas was and the excitement and build up to it. I saw houses with lights on and decorations in the windows and mid-December we got some decorations out of the loft and put a tree up in the house, really, we did, a tree in the house! How silly. The tree was decorated up and it did look nice, especially at night when the main light in the living room was off and the lights on the tree were switched on. I remember sitting at the side of mummy while she was wrapping presents up for people [and for me] and writing cards out. Mummy said they were going to make it an extra special Christmas in 2022 as it was my first proper one. There was a "Santa stop here" sign in the garden and I sat at the side of it, apparently you get presents if you're good. I had to tell him, I'm a Princess now.

Mummy and daddy did some food shopping and when they got home my little nose was on fire! What could I smell? Chicken, beef, oooh it smells lovely, it seems we have that on Christmas Day with lots of different vegetables. Mummy and Storm have Quorn roast but I'm not fussy I'll eat that too; I do love my food. Mummy cooked the meat on Christmas Eve and I can tell you it was the best smell I ever did smell. I just hope I don't have to wait until the next day now to sample it. I struck lucky though cus apparently as a tradition, every Christmas Eve daddy has a beef and mustard sandwich at night "to see if its cooked right" so I knew I'd get some too. Between us that night, we made a start on the beef and I had some chicken too, it was beautiful, now roll on Christmas Day so I can get some more!

Christmas Day started with a walk, I was abit disappointed to be honest with you as I wanted my dinner but I was told I need to build up an appetite and still have my walk. Reece and Storm were still in bed so I went out with mummy and daddy while the two lazy bones kids got up, fancy staying in bed on Christmas Day, even I'm excited now I know all about it. During the walk we saw a few people and swapped "happy Christmas" to them, one man asked me if I was all excited and I thought to myself "well I am a Princess now". I wonder if I'll get my very own crown. To be honest with you I couldn't stop thinking about that beef and chicken, and when it would be going in my belly.

When we got home Reece and Storm were finally up and waiting to open presents, they said we had been out ages and I was really wanting to say that they should have got out of bed earlier. I thought I'd best shush though as I didn't want to be in any bad books before dinner or I might not get any! They all opened their presents and I was abit bewildered as I saw lots of presents on the settee and mummy said they were for me. How do I open them? Mummy took a present to show me and said it was mine, I tried to bite it, well it is mine!

I wasn't able to take the paper off so mummy helped me and I loved what was inside, some treats! Opening more presents and I saw more and more treats, I'm starting to like this Christmas, really, I am! I was overloaded with treats, and overwhelmed too, people really did love me! The only bad thing was that I was only allowed a few of the treats cus mummy didn't want me getting poorly, or fat. I enjoyed a few treats then tried to shove my nose in others before mummy moved them. Now, what times dinner?

Mummy starts preparing and cutting the veg around 11am, we had fresh carrots, cauliflower, broccoli, green beans, parsnips, peas, sprouts, roast and mash potatoes, all smelt lovely. Then you'll never guess what? Mummy said she was having her treat now and poured a glass of wine, really, she did! The stuffing was made too but I wasn't allowed that, I didn't mind as with whatever else there was I think they'd be enough for us 5, the cats and the 10,000 when they arrived. Mummy's glass was empty and daddy asked her "did you spill that?" and mummy cheekily said, "yes down my neck" and then daddy poured her another glass! I hope she can manage to finish the dinner cus by now I'm dribbling, I'm drooling, I'm desperately hungry!

Luckily dinner was ready for around 12.45 and we were all called in the kitchen to see how much we wanted on our plates, or in my case, in my dish. Daddy plated the meat up [I'll have some daddy please, a few right big juicy slices of beef and a few chicken legs, tar]. The veg went on the plates and every time mummy put veg on the plates, she scooped some up to put in my dish. It was covering the meat up but I'd soon sort that out. My dinner didn't last long, now, who's sharing?

After dinner I was still sat waiting for seconds, but they never came, I was told I'd had more than enough and can have some more later. I did sulk, really, I did. Mummy, Reece and Storm took bets on how long it would be after dinner till daddy fell asleep and started snoring, apparently it wasn't that long. They were watching a film and had to turn the sound up to cover daddy's snoring! Do you think they'd notice if I disappeared into the kitchen to find my hidden treats? The answer to that was yes, as soon as I made a move I got asked where I was going and what am I doing? I ended up in my bed sulking.

Supper time was cheese and crackers, that's ok, I love cheese! How much would I get? They all know I love my food. I wasn't allowed any crackers but managed to nab some cheese, and when it was put back in the fridge, I got given some more beef. I wish everyday could be Christmas really, I do. Not that I ever go without but I've never seen as much food and I quite liked it.

Christmas 2023 was near enough the same, I knew what to expect now so was looking forward to all the build-up of it. I helped mummy wrap presents up, I laid on the wrapping paper to keep it safe, I was such a good girl. I got lots of presents again and loads of treats, I did manage to help myself to some this time before they got moved out of my way. I got called a cheeky bugga, I told them, I'm a Princess now and they best not forget it! Daddy fell asleep again, mummy nearly joined him until she jolted herself awake and decided to potter round tidying up all the torn wrapping paper and breaking up boxes. I also helped mummy break the boxes up, I'm such a clever girl, I laid on one and it split open, clever little Princess.

We don't do much New Years Eve, mummy and daddy don't like going out [Reece went out with his friends] so we stayed in with Storm. They always have a takeaway for tea on New Years Eve and I do love kebab what daddy has so I was looking forward to that. I couldn't believe it when daddy decided to have a pizza instead! They'd best be lots of meat on that pizza now daddy cus your girl needs feeding!

That pizza really was nice, or the meat was [daddy said he wouldn't know being as I had most of it] and I really enjoyed some chips and cheese as well. I do love my food! We ended up staying up to see the New Year in then we went to bed, I was happy cus I knew I was in my forever home and I had a full belly.

Fireworks were going off most of the night but they don't bother me, I slept through them but I kept hearing mummy and daddy curse them abit as they went on for too long. New Years Day was quiet and I was hoping mummy would cook again, no such luck, I was on dog food!

CHAPTER 14

FACEBOOK FURRY FRIENDS

Teddy did chapters about the pets on our Facebook page and gave them a mention so I thought it would be good if I did the same. I'm working on the information you told me so some may be more detailed than others. I'm writing your words. At the time of writing also, all information is true, if there's any changes that I get informed of while writing I will correct it but otherwise it's all as you told me. So I'm going to start with the dog category just because the first comment on the Facebook post was from a dog owner. So meet my new friends, I'm such a popular girl!

[Dogs:]

Emma has a beautiful Lurcher cross girl who's 14 and called MELODY. She was adopted from Dogs Trust at 9 weeks old and had a sister called Harmony who they never saw. Melody likes sleeping in the sun. Thank you for being my friend.

Maureen has MAX [Maximoo] a 12 year old tan colour Staffi cross who was adopted at 2 and a half years old after having 4 previous owners and a broken tail. Max has a trapped nerve in his back resulting in weakness in his legs. He's kept as comfy and pain free as possible by the vets and Maureen. Thank you being my friend. [Maureen met Teddy] [since writing this, Max has very sadly joined the rainbow bridge, sleep tight Max].

Marilyn has MISHA a Chocolate Roan Cocker Spaniel who likes watching the tv and doggies on Facebook. Thank you for being my friend.

S Kittycat has SMIRNOFF who is 9 years old and a Chi/JR cross and he's very spoiled but can be lazy. He sleeps most of the day in his fluffy bed under his blanket. Smirnoff has radar ears and is Kittycats shadow. Thank you for being my friend.

Lyndsay has TEDDY who's a Chocolate Miniature Poodle and is 11. He's a character and is very loved and spoiled. Teddy was ill last year and they thought the worse but luckily, he pulled through and thankfully he's fine now. Thank you for being my friend.

Karen has STAR a Jack Russell who's 8 and is very loving, she's a fussy eater and loves going to bed. SKYE who's a Jackawawa and 7, she loves to bark and destroy toys. LEO is 3 and a white Pug, he's very loving but he does pinch his sisters food and treats. [Karen and the 3 dogs met Teddy] Thank you for being my friend.

Anne has SOPHIE who's 13 and she's a German Shepherd / Mastiff and is tan with black flecks down her back, her face is quite grey now. Sophie was rescued as a 16 week old puppy. Thank you for being my friend.

Christine has GEORGE who's 5 and an Orange Roan Cocker Spaniel, he's beautiful and a little bit naughty and is known as Grumpy George. [see also rainbow bridge section]

Renee has LEXI who's very bossy and thinks the field belongs to her and she doesn't like strangers on "her" field. When they do come on the field, she has to go on her lead so the strangers can come on. Thank you for being my friend. [see also rainbow bridge section]

Helen has JAZZ [Jazz monster] who's a Springer Spaniel. She's very special and lives in the moment after having the 2nd 'C' taken out and outlived what the Ologist said. Jazz is looking after her grandma right now who she's not seen for months as she's been in hospital so they both need cuddles. Thank you for being my friend.

Sharon has ORLA a Black and Tan German Shepherd who's a rescue from Croatia, they saw her while on holiday and adopted her. Orla is very gentle and loves kisses but not hugs. Her passport says she's 8 years old. Thank you for being my friend.

Debs has DOTTIE who's a 9 year old Springer Spaniel. Their family always talk about us and are glad I'm writing a book. They say Ted and Roxy would be super proud of us. Thank you for being my friend.

Gillian has TED [fluffy bum or pumpkin] who's 9 and a grey and tan Yorkshire Terrier and he was adopted from a family aged 6. He's a loving boy who's had most of his teeth out and bladder stone removed. Ted is really brave as he never moaned during the scans and x-rays even though he must have been in pain. He's loved to the moon and back. Thank you for being my friend. [see also rainbow bridge section]

Lizzie has her baby girl BRAMBLE who's a brown Cocker Spaniel and 14 months old. She's very bouncy and loves cuddles. Thank you for being my friend.

Gloria has JACK who's 13 and a puppy farm rescue. He had Parvo and 2 cruciate ligaments and thankfully overcame them. He does have Thyroid problems and needs daily medication. Jack is very loving and cuddly and likes his daily walks on the beach. Thank you for being my friend.

Julie has LUCY who's 7 and a Springer Spaniel along with CHARLIE who's also a Springer Spaniel and a year old. Thank you for being my friend.

Teresa has PADDY PAWS and he's 20 months old and a Tri Colour working Cocker Spaniel. He loves to run run run and play with his toys, especially baby squeaky, his kong teddy. Paddy Paws loves cuddles. Thank you for being my friend. [see also rainbow bridge section]

Angela has TIFFANY who's a German Short Haired Pointer. She's mischievous but loveable and likes nothing more than walks with her dad and giving everyone cuddles. Thank you for being my friend. [We met Tiffany and family when we were on holiday].

Lfl has CHINA who's 8 and KAISHI who's 3 and they are both Chuandong Hounds [Chinese Scent Hounds] The breed standard says they must be red in colour with or without a black mask. Thank you for being my friend.

Nanette has ALFIE who's a 12 year old Golden Retriever, he's very loving and quiet and loves everyone. At the moment he's suffering with his back legs but is under the vets care. Thank you for being my friend.

Debra has MILLIE a Romanian rescue who was an hour away from being killed, luckily, she was saved. Debra has had her 4 years now and got her when she lost her beloved Missy [see rainbow bridge section] Thank you for being my friend.

Helen has ALBIE who's a 11 and half year old Apricot Cockerpoo who behaves like a puppy. He loves the beach, paddling and any walk he can get. Albie loves Helens Grandchildren and has great fun with them. He loves his food. Helen and Albie met Ted. Thank you for being my friend.

Cathryn has CHARLIE who's 8 and a Black and White Lhaso Apso. LILY is 6 and a Black and Tan Yorkie who was rescued when her owner didn't want her. DAISY is a Black and Tan Yorkie who's 4. Cathryn and her sister Sylvia met Ted. Thank you for being my friend. [see also rainbow bridge section]

Sheila has a step baby KOPPER who's 4 years old and a black cross between Labrador / Border Collie on his daddy's side and Belgian Malinois / Rottweiler on his mummy's side. We met Kopper in August 2023 in Eyam. Sheila also met Ted. Thank you for being my friend.

Sheila has PEBBLES who is Blue Roan Cocker Spaniel who loves to carry a toy around and is food focused. QUINN is Black with a white patch on his chest and neck and also a Cocker Spaniel who's like a baby and wants tennis balls and permanent fuss. Thank you for being my friend.

Tina has BEAU who she adopted when her mum couldn't care for him during health problems and he adapted straight away. OTIS is a Cocker Spaniel and has just turned a year old, he was bred in Oxford and they first saw him at 4 weeks, he's from a litter of 8 pups and joined their family at 9 weeks old. Thank you for being my friend. We have met Tina, Mark, Beau and Otis. [see also rainbow bridge]

Sue has TEDDY known as TT who's an 8 year old Toy Poodle and was adopted in April 2023. He's a bundle of energy and has filled Sue's life with light again, he's such a treasure. Sue met Teddy. [see also rainbow bridge]

[Cats:]

Teresa has JII-KAHNNAHLEE who is a 5 year old Cream Burmese boy. He's very loving and also very vocal. He's spoilt and naughty and has his humans wrapped round his little paws. Thank you for being my friend.

Margaret has SEBASTIAN and SELENE who are 14 months old and little darlings [monsters] who used the bedroom tv to balance on and had it over, costing £300 for a new one. Thank you for being my friend.

Sharon has TERRI a grey 3 year old and my mummy helped Sharon through a hard time when she wasn't in a good place. Terri is really loved and they wouldn't be without her. Sharon has met little ole me. Thank you for being my friend.

Lin has LUCKY and PRINCE, they've had a hard few years due to changes in the family and lots happening but they are now happy and settled in Cornwall. Lin met Ted. Thank you for being my friend.

Holly has ELVIRA who's 11 years old and black and white. She was adopted from the RSPCA at 3 years old. LUCKY is 19 months old and was found as an 8 week old kitten in their garden. She loves bringing birds, pigeons and toads in the house. Lucky also winds up Elvira and gets told off by her. Thank you for being my friend.

Natalie has OREO who's a 9 year old black and white rescue. She's very loving and loves food. She's the Queen of the close and has everyone wrapped round her paw. Thank you for being my friend.

Rebecca has MILO and JACOB who are ginger and white brothers adopted from Cats Protection 5 years ago. Milo loves playing with milk bottle tops and Jacob likes ripping up cardboard boxes. Thank you for being my friend.

Joyce has HOLLY who is black and white and TIGGER who is a Tabby. Thank you for being my friend.

Ruth has SMOKEY, JASPER and PATCH. Ruth met Ted. Thank you for being my friend. [see also rainbow bridge]

Carol has BEE a Domestic black cat who has kept her strong this last two or so years and is her best friend. Thank you for being my friend.

Sue has JAFFA who's 8 and a Cream British Short haired chunky boy who's very laid back. WILLOW is grey and white, 13 and half years old and very demanding. She thinks she's top cat. Thank you being my friend. [see also rainbow bridge section]

Maureen has BILLY BOB a Tuxedo rescue boy who needed an indoor home with no other cats. Maureen's previous boy [see rainbow bridge] had a hand in Tuxedo being rescued. Thank you for being my friend.

[Families:]

Julie has DILL a 6 year old Springer Spaniel who has done obedience to platinum level, he's also done mantrailling and scentwork. Dill has his own Facebook page. DUSTIN is a 10 year old Tabby and white cat, he's very sweet but not that bright. CLEO is a dilute Tortie of 14 years but looks like a kitten. She was rescued off Preloved and at 8 months old had already had a litter, her owners gave her away. TOFFEE is Ginger and treats his owners like his personal slaves. They got him 12 years ago when he was thrown out with his brother as they didn't get on with 2 puppies. Thank you for being my friend. [see also rainbow bridge]

Jennie has OBI who she's just rehomed at 8 years old, he's a Springer Spaniel. PAWLIE and LOUIE are her daughters cats, Pawlie is 6/7 years old and Louie is 5 months. Thank you for being my friend. [see also rainbow bridge]

Yvette has KRISTOFF a 9 year old black Cockapoo boy who loves cuddles and his ball. He puts up with his little sister and has been known to sit on her when she's being annoying. But he does like to play with her and cuddle her sometimes. KYRA is also a black Cockerpoo and is 4 years old and for the first 18 months she was known as "devil child" as she would bite anyone and anything and liked human flesh. She's calmed down now and has the sweetest way of giving hugs and kisses. Despite being small she can carry things across the floor from her toy box, she adores her big brother. CHESNEY [aka Sir Chesney] is a 12 year old Bengal cat he's stunningly gorgeous, affectionate, clever, has huge back feet and he's so smart he joins in on local dog walks. He doesn't like Kyra very much but tolerates Kristoff. Thank you for being my friend.

[Other pets]

Mandy has ROSIE who is a lone Guinea pig since losing sisters AVRO and DELTA. Rosie is 5 years old and is really cheeky but loving and taken on her sister's ways. She loves a trip to the shops in her pink stroller. Thank you for being my friend. [Since writing this, Rosie very sadly crossed to Rainbow bridge]

Right this is the Rainbow bridge section and it was hard to write so it's going to be hard to read, especially if you wanted your own baby mentioned. Get tissues, get a drink, get settled, here we go.

[Rainbow bridge:]

Julie sadly lost LAIKA a beautiful ginger girl cat who was 11 years old when she was taken by cancer. BADGER was a Tuxedo boy who was half Siamese and was taken at age 15 and a half. You're both very sadly missed and we hope you found Ted and Roxy. Sweet babies rest peacefully. We love you. [see also family section]

Christine sadly lost BEN and JETT two beautiful black Cocker Spaniels who left her 5 years ago but she misses them every day. You're both very sadly missed and we hope you found Ted and Roxy. Sweet babies rest peacefully. We love you. [see also dog section]

Dawn sadly lost LUCKY and TARA who were both German Shepherds and they are missed every day. Tara left her aged 13 and Lucky was 12 and was Dawns soulmate. You're both very sadly missed and we hope you found Ted and Roxy. Sweet babies rest peacefully. We love you.

Renee sadly lost ROXIE to a tumour, Roxie was in Ted's book. You're very sadly missed and we hope you found

Ted and Roxy. Sweet baby rest peacefully. We love you. [see also dog section]

Jennie sadly lost LAYLA LO LO and BUSTER BOO, they were both rescued Springer Spaniels. Boo was a year old when rescued, Lo was 6 months. You're both very sadly missed and we hope you found Ted and Roxy. Sweet babies rest peacefully. We love you. [see also dog section]

Gillian very sadly lost Ted a Yorkshire Terrier in 2017 aged 10. He was a dear companion when his daddy died suddenly in 2009. Ted was adopted at 9 months old in 2007 and was one of 92 dogs rescued from a house. He was nearly blind before he left Gill. You're very sadly missed and we hope you found our Ted and Roxy. Sweet baby rest peacefully. We love you. [see also dog section]

Susan sadly lost SCRUFFY who was rescued from barbed wire in the woods when they lived in Cyprus. He was approximately 4 months old and was rescued with a bigger dog living in the woods [he got rehomed]. He came to live with Sue in the UK on a pet passport when he was 5. Aged 2 he was diagnosed with Addisons disease but thanks to a very good vet and life medication he lived to be 18 and a half though he was deaf and blind. They have his ashes to be scattered with Sue and hubby when it's their time. You're very sadly missed and we hope you found Ted and Roxy. Sweet baby rest peacefully. We love you. Susan met Ted.

Andrew sadly lost his angel son JACK a black and white Staffie crossed labrador. He loved stealing food and was 12 and a half when he left Andrew. His twin sister JILLIAN LOUISE was a brown and white version of him who was calm and chilled out, she was 16 and a half when she left Andrew, they were both rescued at 3-4 weeks. His son MAX was a big red Pitbull who has been abused before he got him, he was brave and kind and adored everyone, he left Andrew aged 19. Son OSCAR was a black Toy Poodle who had a cheeky bark and used to stand on the top of the bath and drink from the sink. He left Andrew aged 16 and a half. They all rescued Andrew and he tries every day to repay them. You're all very sadly missed and we hope you found Ted and Roxy. Sweet babies rest peacefully. We love you.

Ruth sadly lost DAI [David in Welsh] KIP and TAFFY. They were all German Shepherds and dearly loved. You're all sadly missed and we hope you found Ted and Roxy. Sweet babies rest peacefully. We love you. [see also cat section] Ruth met Ted.

Sandy sadly lost KAZZ in September 2023 aged nearly 14 and misses her very much. You're sadly missed and we hope you found Ted and Roxy. Sweet baby rest peacefully. We love you.

Debra sadly lost her dog MISSY who she'll never get over. She helped Debra when she lost her mum and suffered panic attacks and had a breakdown. She lost Missy a day after her 14th birthday. You're sadly missed and we hope you found Ted and Roxy. Sweet baby rest peacefully. We love you. [see also dog section]

Cathryn sadly lost her angel Westie MACKENZIE and her little ELLIE MAY at 10 weeks who was also a Westie. You're sadly missed and we hope you found Ted and Roxy. Sweet babies rest peacefully. We love you. [see also dog section]

Valerie sadly lost GEMMA a 16 year old Tortie and white cat who was rescued as a feral kitten and became her soulmate. She sadly lost a battle to cancer and she's carried in Valeries heart. You're sadly missed and we hope you found Ted and Roxy. Sweet baby rest peacefully. We love you.

Teresa sadly lost SAMUEL 3 years ago, he was a Liver and white Springer Spaniel baby. His fave things were his kongs and crispy brown leaves. Teresa talks to him every day and misses him so much. You're sadly missed and we hope you found Ted and Roxy. Sweet baby rest peacefully. We love you. [see also dog section]

Andrea sadly lost DOTTIE in April 2023, she was a 12 year old Westie Cross and she's missed so very much. You're sadly missed and we hope you found Ted and Roxy. Sweet baby rest peacefully. We love you.

Maureen sadly lost BUBLE, named after the singer Michael, he was a beautiful Lilac British short haired pedigree cat who sadly passed on Maureen's Grand-son's birthday. He was the first pedigree after so many rescues. You're sadly missed and we hope you found Ted and Roxy. Sweet baby rest peacefully. We love you. [see also dog section]

Jasmine sadly lost cats CHARLIE and WINNIE who were like an old married couple. If one of the cats was outdoors and the other one was indoors, the one indoors would sit fretting at the door for the other one. Charlie would sit back and let Winnie eat first. You're both sadly missed and we hope you have found Ted and Roxy. Sweet babies rest peacefully. We love you.

Julia sadly lost MAX and BEN in 2016, Ben was a Black Labrador and Max was a Chocolate Labrador and both are missed each day. You're both sadly missed and we hope you found Ted and Roxy. Sweet babies rest peacefully. We love you.

Jo sadly lost her sexy boy DRESDEN in 2019 who was 9 years old and a beautiful fluffy cat. He used to bring Jo cat toys and miaow all the way down the hall to let her know he was bringing one. Every evening he would wait on an ottoman they had in the hallway for a stroke and kiss goodnight before bed. You're sadly missed and we hope you found Ted and Roxy. Sweet baby rest peacefully. We love you.

Sue sadly lost DAISY a 4 year old Golden Tabby cat who was the sweetest girl with a squeak for a miaow who is missed and loved very much. You're sadly missed and we hope you found Ted and Roxy. Sweet baby rest peacefully. We love you. [see also cat section]

Amanda sadly lost HARVEY a gorgeous little white and brown Rough Coated Terrier, he was also mentioned in Teddy's book. You're sadly missed and we hope you found Ted and Roxy. Sweet baby rest peacefully. We love you.

Tina sadly lost BAILEY who was a Cocker Spaniel and a friend of Teddy's, he was 8 years old. Bailey suddenly became ill and unfortunately lost his fight. You're sadly missed and we hope you found Ted and Roxy. Sweet baby rest peacefully. We love you.

Sue sadly lost JACKSON who was a Pug and only with Sue for 14 months before sadly losing his battle with illness on Valentines Day 2023 and he's such a loss. You're sadly missed and we hope you found Ted and Roxy. Sweet baby rest peacefully. We love you.

So there we are, all my new friends, sadly some as above, aren't here with us now but we love them all. Thank you to all my friends for making me feel welcome and wanting a mention in my book. It's been an honour to include you and I've enjoyed learning all about you. Love n stuff, your friend Ruby XXxxXXxx

CHAPTER 15

SPIKE

I think most of you know about my mate Spike who lives next door, well he was really good friends with Teddy firstly and he used to come round to play with him. Teddy taught Spike all about his babbies and how to carry them round in his mouth. We still have Teddy's babbies in his toy boxes round the house and Spike will play with them, he's brought a few of his own round too. Usually by the time he goes back home there's a pile of them on the settee like he's had a party, he sometimes puts them in my bed, mummy has to move them before I can get in it. He doesn't carry them outside on his walks with him like Teddy did but he does carry them round the house and up the garden [rarely fetches them back in] but he's a good lad and we all love him.

I first met Spike on the day I was adopted, mummy asked his daddy to come round to our house so we could meet, because we have Spike a lot when his daddy's working so it's important that we get on. The first meeting went well, he was sniffing me and I was sniffing him, I probably did stink to be fair but we were getting to know each other. Mummy was looking after Spike the next day as his daddy would be at work so it was a positive start that we got on. Last year his daddy hurt his leg and wasn't able to take Spike out for his walks when he finished work so we started to take him in the mornings when I went for my walk so we ended up going together.

We didn't only go on local walks we went in the car to some places too and it's really funny as when Spikes in the car he's very vocal and makes some really funny noises. It's almost like he's talking sometimes and the noises sound like words, mummy and daddy do laugh at him. He's a lovable lad and when he's with us he don't leave my mummy alone, he'll sit with / on mummy and he stares at her so lovingly. [I do remind him sometimes that she's my mummy and he only borrows her] When we are out on our walks, he's really good and obedient, when he gets called back he comes straight back to us. Sometimes we have a little game where one of us will try to get in front of the other one then give each other a nudge, sort of like a "na na na na na I'm in front" sort of thing. It's all in fun and we have a good time.

When Spikes daddy's leg was better, we still took Spike out on our walks with us as by now he was in the routine and enjoyed his morning walks.

Mummy used to take Spike home after the walks if his daddy wasn't working, and I'd go with them and get a treat from his daddy. The trouble was, when we dropped him off and went to leave to go home, Spike was out of the door and back at our house quicker than we were! So now when we've been out walking, we just take him back to our house and let his daddy pick him up [sometimes he works from home so collects him when he's finished his work]. It's funny too, as Spike will run to our gate after our walk, wanting to stay with us, regardless of if he was expected home or not. In a morning if mummy's not been round next door to collect him as quick as he'd like, Spike will sit in his front garden looking up at our window barking for mummy to collect him. The easy way to do this is for Spikes daddy to open their gate to let him out while mummy goes out to open ours and he can come straight through! He's a right lad I tell ya! I used to love going next door for my treats but I do still get some treats now, I go to the fence and stick my pretty little nose through, then his daddy feeds me treats through the gap. I do like them, and I'm partial to a finger or two as well as I don't always take treats so nicely! I do like my food. You'll have heard the saying "the grass is always greener on the other side?" well I've a new one for you, "the treats always taste better next door".

On the days mummy does go to collect Spike in a morning, daddy puts me in my harness and we meet at the bottom of the steps for our walk. When mummy goes in the house Spike is always waiting for her then she has to wait a few minutes for him to calm down before she can put his collar on as he's always so excited. He does love jumping up at my mummy. And Spike knows mummy as "Auntie Trace".

For those of you who don't know, Spike is a white Staffi with a black patch on his face and a black spot on his back. He's a rescue like me and his daddy says he thinks he was around 3/4 years old when he adopted him but the vet said he was closer to aged 6/7. So we're not really sure how old he is, he could now be 9/10 or around 13. Either way he's a good runner and always bouncy, and really lively. He loves his walks with us and it's company for both of us, he loves coming round!

He always sits as close as he can to mummy when she sits down and always nudges her arm with his nose so she can put her arm round him. He follows mummy all over, and though he likes being with all of us and loves being stroked, he will wait outside the bathroom door for mummy.

We went to York a few weeks ago to see Storm and we took Spike with us. Each other time we've been without him, I've gone into the accommodation and gone in Storm's room and none of the staff have known I was in there. When we went in with Spike, he started barking and the staff heard him and we got thrown out! Hahaha! We've not been back in there since, me and Spike wait outside with daddy when mummy goes into Storm's room now. He's a funny lad, he really is.

Oh, just one more thing, we are just mates, best mates, best buddies, best friends, there's no romance at all, really there isn't! We do get called boyfriend and girlfriend but honestly, we're just two dogs who happen to be a boy and a girl [Princess, if you don't mind] and best friends at that.

CHAPTER 16

DADDY'S 70TH AND ALL THEM STEPS

Daddy's 70th birthday was coming up and mummy wanted to treat him and do something special to involve me [cus I'm a Princess now]. Mummy thought long and hard and believe me we did hear mummy's brain rattling quite a lot! Then mummy had an idea, [I'm told she does have them occasionally] and asked daddy if he fancied going back to the Lake District. You see, they had part of their honeymoon there and though they went back a few times after that, they hadn't been in years even though they had spoken about it. Daddy said it was a lovely idea and to look into it, so mummy started to look for places to stay, luckily most of it was dog friendly. Mummy found a pub just outside of Kendall that offered accommodation and looked lovely, it was dog friendly so she booked it for 3 nights. Some of you may know that Teddy's birthday is the day before daddy's and it was on the 7th March as Teddy would have turned 9 that we set off to the Lakes for a few days.

We couldn't check in to the pub until 3pm and we didn't want to waste a day so we set off midmorning and drove to Lake Windermere first. It was lovely, I had a right good time, I didn't chase any of the birds as I don't really play but daddy let me off my lead in a small area that was safe and I had a little sniff and wander around. Mummy and daddy were talking about a pub they stayed in when they came on honeymoon and wanted to find it. Mummy said if she hadn't been so dopey, she should have booked to stay in this pub but none of them can remember what it's called! They remember where it was though and we walked straight to it and it was exactly how they remembered it. The accommodation was a separate part of it and sat to the side and it looked lovely, but we'd already booked to stay somewhere else. We did go in for a drink though and the first thing I saw when we walked in was a jar full of dog treats just for me! Mummy and daddy were sat with a drink and I was munching on the handful of treats mummy had got for me while still watching that treat jar hoping for some more! Mummy said I couldn't have too many as the other visiting dogs would have some and I'd get a tummy ache. It wasn't what I wanted to hear as I do like my food!

When it was time to drive to where we were staying, we set off and it was only 15 minutes away. When we got there it looked lovely but it was quite out of the way, no other pubs around and just a few houses. We parked the car up and went inside, to say it was out of the way it seemed a popular place as plenty of people were in there. We told the lady behind the bar we had a room booked for a few days and she got the keys to check us in to our room, what we didn't know was the steps we had passed by in the car park were the steps up to the rooms. They were old metal steps with gaps that you could see through and I didn't like them as soon as I saw them. The lady went up the steps and mummy followed, I didn't follow, I didn't like the steps. Daddy had to help me up them by lifting me with my harness and keeping me safe. We were shown to our room and it was lovely, but what I didn't tell you was that mummy forget to bring one of my beds, really, she did! 3 beds and she didn't bring any of them, and I tell you after walking up all those bloody steps I'll need a lie down!

Mummy and daddy said that being as there were no other pubs in walking distance that we were going to stay here today, have some drinks in the bar and relax. That suited me as I was tired and I didn't really want to go gallivanting off, we've the next few days to do that. They did some unpacking and put some things where they needed to be, they couldn't put my bed anywhere being as they forgot to bring one! I did find myself a nice little comfy spot though to settle down in. No sooner had I settled down I hears "Rube come on darling, are we going downstairs?" So it looks like my cosy little spot will have to wait til later, now let's get to the bar, down all them bloody steps! Daddy had to help me again, I really didn't like them at all, there'd best be a treat for me when we get to that bar!

The bar had emptied out since we had checked in and we had a choice of seats, we sat near the window and I laid down. Mummy went to the bar then my eyes were on stalks, what did I see? Treats, treats and more treats! Mummy brought me some over, then guess what? The nice lady who shown us to our room made a beeline for me with a handful of treats! She's my new best friend as every time she passed me that weekend, she stroked me and made a fuss of me, and most importantly she kept bringing me treats! Mummy and daddy booked a table that night to eat in the pub, daddy wouldn't be able to drive after having some drinks and there wasn't anywhere close enough to get food, it suited me again as I didn't have to go anywhere and I knew I'd get fed! I'd already spotted the cabinet in the corner with dog "meals" in it and I had my eye on the big one, "doggie fish chips and peas" I think I'll enjoy that one! I knew as well that I'd get some of whatever daddy orders so my belly will be full tonight.

Tea was lovely, daddy ordered the pie so I had lots of juicy steak [daddy said the crust was nice hehehe] and I did take myself over to the cabinet to show mummy the doggy meals. It didn't take long til she had asked the lady to give me the fish, chips and peas, turns out the fish were sprats, the chips were treats shaped as chips and the peas were round green treats, I'm not bothered, I got my belly fed! We had a few drinks after tea and decided to go to bed and see what was on telly, [proper rock and roll us]. As we were leaving the bar, we saw fluffy blankets in a corner that were free to borrow but must be returned, so mummy grabbed two for me to sleep on, I should think so too, being as she forgot my bed! The only thing now was …. All them bloody steps!

I slept well to say that mummy forgot my bed [I'm not forgetting that hehehe] but I did take myself off into the bathroom during the night to sleep on the cool floor. Mummy and daddy kept saying that it was my choice to lay there and I was happy enough, each time they came

122

into the bathroom I wagged my tail and lifted my paw up for a belly rub.

It was daddy's birthday the next day and mummy had brought his cards and presents away with us and he opened them before breakfast. I bought him a book he wanted cus I'm a really good girl and I got lots of cuddles. When it was time for breakfast, we made our way down all them bloody steps! Daddy had to lift me this time as I wasn't moving, I didn't like the steps and I wasn't going down them, not even breakfast tempted me. We had a stroll round the car park til it was time to go in and what did we see? A beautiful robin, really, we did! There was no sign of Teddy yesterday on his birthday so mummy was happy to see the robin today, then you'll never believe this, a single white feather did come floating down out of nowhere and land at mummy's feet! Hello Ted. The reason we didn't have any sign of Ted on his birthday is cus he was helping Shell and Bruces mummy, Lily over the Rainbow Bridge. Lily sadly left us on Teddys birthday and he was there guiding her safely on her journey. Ted met Lily and she did love him, Bruce has his own chapter in Ted's first book, they a very special little family.

I'm a right charmer, really, I am. I got my very own sausage at breakfast time brought out by the chef himself! He heard there was a Princess staying in the pub and wanted to meet me! I had my own sausage before they even asked mummy and daddy what they wanted! I did get some of daddy's breakfast too and listen to this, when all the other people had been fed there was some black pudding left, guess who's belly that went in!!!

We went to Keswick for the day to have a look round and to find the statue of Max the wonder dog, he's like Teddy, he did lots of fundraising and sadly passed. He's got his own statue in memory of him that a lot of people go to visit. It was a long drive so I slept all the way as I knew I'd have to save my strength for later when we walked round. The funniest and best part of the day was when daddy had let me off my lead in the park and mummy didn't know. We'd been talking to someone with a Springer and of course mummy was lagging behind as she was fussing the dog [even though mummy had Ted and has got me she's a sucker for a Springer] Anyway when mummy finally caught us up, I went trotting, off lead down to meet her, mummy was nearly crying, really, she was, "awwww baby girl are you off your lead and come to surprise mummy?". I did smile when she saw me, mummy did too, it was a lovely surprise and daddy was stood behind smiling.

We found Max's bench and statue and had some photo's took, it was a lovely warm day so we had a walk round the park, me like a big girl off my lead, well what's a Princess to do? We called for some chips after we left the park, we weren't eating at the pub tonight as we were meeting friends. I got a lovely sausage, some of mummy's chips and some of daddy's chips. I'll walk it all off over the next few days and anyway, I'm on holiday. We left Keswick ready to go back to the pub to meet mummy's friends, we had a lovely day, I'm ready for a nap though now.

When we got back to the pub, daddy mentioned about going back to the room for an hour before we met up with Edwina and Brian but mummy said about those bloody steps and I'd have to go up and down them within an hour. We decided to sit in the bar [it was a really really tough decision .....] and have a few drinks before we met them. Edwina is in team TeddyRoxyRuby and is a massive Teddy fan, we've never met before and unfortunately, she never met Ted. We'd arranged to meet at 5pm and luckily there was a table with 4 chairs available so we nabbed it ready for when they arrived. They were a lovely couple, Edwina greeted mummy with a massive hug and smile and I got called a beautiful Princess. We had a few drinks and there were lots of laughs, Edwina really regretted not meeting Teddy but was happy to meet me cus I'm a Princess now. They stayed with us for a few hours before it was time to leave, it was getting dark and the road to and from the pub was narrow and bumpy so we needed to make sure they got off safely. We had a lovely time and it was lovely to meet them. We spent the rest of the night in the bar before we went back to the room up all those bloody steps!

The next day, Saturday, I had to be carried down all them bloody steps again so we could have breakfast. It was worth it though as again, I was the first fed, I was told that as there were more people staying at the pub, there were no spare sausages but I did get lots of black pudding! Mummy saw they had fresh croissants on the cereal bar and went to get one, she'd not even buttered it when my nose started twitching and I parked myself at the side of her for some. Did you know warm croissant is lovely? I know now, mummy doesn't hehe! I got some of daddy's breakfast as well and the lady I made friends with who worked there brought me out a rasher of bacon! Now, what times dinner? I do love my food.

We went to Ambleside for the day and we nearly got lost finding the car on the way back really, we did. We parked up in a car park near a boys football ground and had a longish walk in to the town centre where we wanted to be. Ambleside was lovely, mummy loved some of the shops and bought some things for Teddy and Roxy's Garden. We had a lovely walk round and spent ages there, I think I'd charmed everyone there as they were all saying how gorgeous I am. As we were leaving, we couldn't remember how to get back to the car, as I said we had a long walk and silly mummy and daddy couldn't remember which way we needed to be! Eventually we found the right way and after about 3 days [hehehe] we made our way back to the car.

We decided to go back to Lake Windermere as when we went on the first day we arrived we didn't go to the shops, the rain had dried up by now and the sun was shining so mummy had shopping fever. We managed to get the last car park space in the car park near the shops and you'll never believe what we saw …… lots of Springer Spaniels! Really, there were loads, I mean there were none as cute as me but you'd know that. One of the shops sold lots of animal stuff so mummy was straight in, I was stood with my nose to the window looking what she was buying me. When she came out of the shop she had the tiniest bag, well you can't fit many treats in that mummy!! What I hadn't seen was that mummy's hoodie pocket looked really packed and when I had a closer look, my nose wafted as well, treats!!! Thanks mummy.

We walked back round to the pub again that we went to the other day where mummy and daddy stayed all those years ago. It was still warm and dry so we sat outside, mummy was smiling at another dog, she does that a lot, and the dog's owner started talking, it turns out they had another dog under the table that mummy hadn't seen. She put this really silly voice on when she talks to dogs, really, she does, and the dogs look at her like she's crackers [she really is]. All I was bothered about was getting more treats as I remembered they had some inside the pub but mummy said I'd had enough, think I ought to tell her she's had enough beer, see how she likes it!!

We made our way back to the pub we were staying in and we were eating there again. That's ok as I hadn't quite emptied that doggy treat cupboard out yet so I'll be looking forward to that. When we got back, the pub was packed, there were some village events going off and the pub seemed the place to be. We were thinking of going back to the room again but thought of them bloody steps! So we decided to stay downstairs for a few drinks before tea and hope it clears out abit, it didn't but a few people stood outside so it made it abit calmer.

Tea was nice, I know as I sampled some of daddy's, some of mummy's and had my own out of the doggy treat cupboard, talking of that cupboard, I think they need to fill it back up as I nearly emptied it all out. After tea we had a few hours in the bar and it got abit rowdy, the people who had been in the bar all afternoon were drunk and being loud, not a problem really till someone stepped back and stood on me. Mummy had been watching him as he kept stumbling about and eventually, he stumbled a step too far and stood on me and kicked me and he didn't even realise. Mummy tapped him on the shoulder and told him what he'd done, he said sorry then started being abit cocky with his mates, saying things like "did you see me step on that dog?" while laughing, he wasn't laughing when he saw mummy looking at him with "that" look on her face. The fella and his mates moved to the other end of the bar.

We went up all them bloody steps to get back to the room to go to bed, as soon as I was in the room I settled myself down, I was shattered. I ended up on the bathroom floor again, it's nice and cool in there and I got myself comfy. I didn't even move when mummy or daddy needed to use the bathroom, except my paw, I lifted my paw up for a rub, well it's hard work being a Princess.

Sunday and I was up early, I needed to do my business so we went down to the car park down all them bloody steps! It was about half hour before it was time for breakfast and I didn't want to walk up those steps again to go back to the room, mummy suggested that she go back to the room to make a hot drink while me and daddy stayed down in the car park. Mummy came down the steps carrying two drinks, granted she spilt most of them but managed to salvage a few mouths full. I was happy in the car park, it wasn't the nicest weather, but it was dry and I was happy sat having a nosey round, that's when we saw the beautiful Robin again, morning Teddy.

When it was time for breakfast I was excited and wondering what I was having from the staff this morning, sausage? black pudding? bacon? I'm not fussy really, I do like my food. I did get some of everything. It was the day we were going home and mummy and daddy were discussing if to go straight home or call off somewhere else for a few hours and were googling places nearby that we hadn't visited. The other option was to head home and if they saw a place that looked interesting, then to park up and have a walk round. The decision ended up being taken away from us anyway, as by the time we'd finished breakfast, paid for the stay and packed up the car, the heavens had opened and the rain was throwing it down so much we got soaked just getting to the car. I'd had a really lovely few days away, now I was ready to go home and go to bed, a bed mummy forgot to pack and take with us.

I won't let mummy forget about my bed even though I didn't need it. Best thing is, when mummy packs to go away she always writes a list of what to take, and yes, my bed was on that list! I'm just glad they remembered to bring me back, hahaha, they didn't have much choice to be fair, I guessed we were going home when they were packing the case, [I'm really clever] so I started doing my spins round the bedroom in excitement of going home after a lovely few days away ..... to my 3 beds.

Not only did daddy go back to the Lake District for the first time in years, he had the honour of not only taking me and spending time with his Princess, he carried me up and down all them bloody stairs!

CHAPTER 17

Tattershall Lakes

[mummy's 50th … mmmm 53rd birthday]

I'm getting older and my illnesses are getting more apparent, I'm coughing more, that's my leaky heart valve, along my cancer and whatever else I have going off. My legs are also not that good, my back ones sometimes give up on me but after I've walked for a while they seem abit better. That's my arthritis, I've got that in my spine and legs, but apart from that I'm good. I've still got an appetite, I do love my food, and I love life. I'm not ready to give up yet, I've too much to do and too much to see, I love my life now and I love my family, more importantly, they love me. One thing that worried mummy and daddy though, was that I can't walk far before I got tired and they knew I loved the outdoors.

We had an upcoming holiday to Tattershall Lakes and mummy and daddy were worried about all the walking I'd have to do. Even though it was a relaxing place we would be visiting the coast and going to the club house at night so they wanted to make sure I wouldn't get too tired. Mummy had the idea of getting me a doggy pram, well I am a baby! Then they joked the pram would be a carriage, well I am a Princess! So a few days later my carriage arrived! Some kind Team TeddyRoxyRuby members donated towards the pram so mummy could get me a bigger one so I'd have more room and wasn't squashed up and uncomfortable. When it arrived, I looked at it and thought to myself, "you're not going to get me in there!", they left it in the kitchen and put some treats in it, in the hope I'd climb in, no I don't think so.

On Sunday we went out for a walk near where we live and I slowed down and got very tired, mummy was pushing the pram and I decided to give it a go and sit in it. Ooooh, it were lovely, really it were! So comfy, so nice, just the right thing for a Princess. And did I feel good being pushed around in my carriage, I only needed a tiara now and I'd be sorted! I really loved it and that proved to mummy and daddy they had done the right thing by getting it for me and they knew I wouldn't struggle when we were away. I had a few days to get used to it before we went on our holibobs and it was good as I knew when I needed to get in it for a rest and when I wanted to come back out.

We arrived in Tattershall Lakes on the Friday 17th May, we had an early check in so we could get everything [except my Princess carriage] out of the car. We usually go to Woodhall Spa first and leave the luggage in the car but we always worry that the car would get smashed so we decided to drive to Woodhall after we'd checked in at Tattershall. We found our lodge, which was funny, haha cus it happened that we turned up at the wrong one, really we did! Storm was trying the key in the lodge door and it wouldn't open, we did wonder why! Haha it was the wrong lodge! It's a good job no one was in it or they be thinking we were on the rob! We found our own lodge which was just around the corner, apparently we were looking for Woodland Way not Woodland retreat. Silly billies!!!

We got all the stuff out of the car that we needed to, beer, food, beer, my beds, my food, beer, the cases, beer, toiletries, beer, cleaning stuff, beer. I had a quick look round and when my bed was down in the living area I climbed in it. The other bed went in the bedroom but I've never even been in the bedroom, really I haven't! But it's there if I need it anytime. At night I've been sleeping in my living room bed, I'm too comfy to disturb so they leave me there but leave the lights on so I can see where I am when I wake up, and mummy and daddy's bedroom door is left wide open so I can see where they are and take myself in if I want to. Also they all check on me during the night, apparently, I'm always snoring away, I don't believe that for a minute! One Princess does not snore!

We've had so much fun this week and been to so many seaside's, Saturday was mummy's birthday she was 53, ermm I mean 50, and we went to the club house for breakfast. I knew I'd get some of daddy's breakfast and my belly was rumbling away. Last time we came here they did a massive breakfast that me and daddy shared but this time it wasn't on the menu so we ordered a normal sized breakfast and daddy was hoping that I'd let him have some, I do like my food! Mummy ordered extra toast that they actually put on daddy's plate, that meant mummy wouldn't eat it as it had been placed on top of the bacon [mummy's a veggie] so that meant more toast for daddy so hopefully more bacon and sausage for me! I did get a fair share to be honest with you, daddy was thankful for the extra toast, mummy wasn't, being as she didn't have any. Oh well, I got my belly full!

We had a walk round afterwards to walk our breakfast off, that's good cus if I walk my breakfast off I'll be ready for my dinner soon enough. On mummy's birthday we went to Chapel St. Lenards and did some shopping. Every time we passed a chippy I tried to pull to go in for a sausage but apparently I'd had enough. It seemed really strange not going to the chippy for dinner as that's what we always do when we come here, but being as we'd been for breakfast, we weren't going, just cus they didn't want anything doesn't mean I don't. I went in my pram for a while as I was getting tired and needed a rest, I was wheeled up to the beach but the sea was right far away and I wasn't bothered to walk that far, but what I did see was a shop that sold ice cream, now that I did want! I saw mummy walk up a ramp and it turns out she was getting tea and coffee to sit on the sea front with, when I saw her coming back down the ramp empty handed, I wondered in all the world of Princess's what was going off. Mummy told daddy that she had ordered the drinks and they poured them into normal cups not takeaway ones so we had to drink them outside the café. By this time I was out of my pram and I did do a little trot up the ramp, they did laugh at me! I was right to run up the ramp though because when we got to the table they were sat at, I was told mummy had ordered me some sausages! They were lovely too, and the lady in the café was saying how beautiful I was and asked how old I was. Daddy told the lady the story of my background and she said how cruel some people are and how lucky I am now. I was hoping the sad story would make the lady give me another sausage, it didn't, but she did open the dog treat tin and give me a few treats.

We had a few seaside trips that week and I really enjoyed them all, I walked for a while then had a ride in my Princess carriage so I got best of both worlds cus I could be nosey and watch the world go by when I was being pushed around. When we went to Mablethorpe I went on the beach and did I enjoy it! Mummy filmed me on her phone while I was trotting off and having fun, I did run the other way after though and make daddy chase me to get me back on the lead! Cheeky Princess. We had a fun day then went to a café for a sandwich, it was dog friendly and there was plenty of space for my carriage. I got two dog sausages too, really, I did! I'll look like a sausage by the time I get home, I'm not bothered though, I do like my food.

We went to the club house a few afternoons / nights for an hour and one time I was surprised by what I thought was mummy's wine, turns out it was doggy wine! It was nice too, I wasn't sure when I first started drinking it as I thought it was water as it was clear, as I had a few more licks I realised it was wine, and I'm only 13 hehehe! Good job it wasn't really wine cus I'd be in bother; I'd definitely need my carriage home if it was real! They sell all sorts now, doggy white wine, doggy rose wine, doggy beer, wonder which I'll try next time. Oh and I even had a doggy ice cream in a tub, I had to wait for it to melt though as it was sticking to my tongue but once it melted it was lovely.

We did spend a lot of time in the lodge as well, some days we got back to the lodge around 5 and decided to stay in, mainly cos of me, they didn't want to take me out unnecessarily after a day out and tire me out so we stayed in so I could rest for the next day. Mummy ended up being full of cold as well and had a sore throat, and a few days in daddy didn't feel well. It always happens when your away doesn't it? Someone not feeling well? They didn't let it spoil things though, we did go out each day. To be honest with you as well I was ready for a sleep when I got in each time, I do remember one time we were out in the day and then went to the club house, that I was fast asleep in my pram for two hours! Two hours! In all the world of Princess's can you believe I slept for two hours in my pram? Erm, sorry, carriage.

There's a pub not far from Tattershall called The Blue Bell and it's centred around The Dam busters 617 squadron, it's been ran as a tribute pub and a lot of memorabilia is on the walls and there's signatures on the ceiling. Anyway, daddy always wanted to go so we went in one day and we were meeting mummy's friend Angela there, they've not met before but talk on messenger and Angela is in the TeamTeddyRoxyRuby. We had a lovely few hours with Angela, her husband Russ and their beautiful dog Tiffany. She was fussy and she's a proper daddy's girl. They bought me some lovely treats too and I did share a few with Tiffany. We went to the

Blue Bell again after we got back from Mablethorpe and daddy had a good look round at all the photos and signatures. Oh and on the way to meet Angela, we took a wrong turning and a 5 minute drive to the pub took 25 minutes! After putting the sat nav on, we again missed another turning, daddy said it gave the direction too late for him to make the turn, I just think he weren't listening hehehe.

Going back to when we went to Woodhall Spa, mummy got sandwiches for everyone and of course I couldn't be left out, I got two big, lovely pieces of ham, it was so delicious! I was in my Princess carriage so I ate it in comfort and yes, I did expect some of the sandwiches too! I got some cheese, it was grated so some fell out of the sandwiches, lovely it was too!

I got lots of attention, in and out of my carriage, while we were out and about. People saying how beautiful I am and what a fantastic life I have now. We saw so many dogs in prams that week, mummy said she's never noticed so many before, maybe it's cus I was in one but there was literally so many. And one dog had the exact same pram as me too! In the club house one night, we saw another Springer in a pram, she was tiny though, [I'm saying she, as the pram was pink, I know we shouldn't speculate these days but that's just how we took it]. Mummy was itching to speak to the lady the dog was with but she wasn't able to as there were too many people around. When we were on the way back from the club house to the lodge one day, we had to move aside for another pram coming towards us, a human baby pram, not a dog. Anyway, as the lady pushing the pram walked past, she looked at me and said "oh I thought it was a baby", mummy said "she is, she's my baby".

We were booked to stay til the 25th ^{of} May, which mummy thought for some reason was the Sunday not the Saturday. We didn't do much the Friday and stayed in the lodge from teatime as we said we would make the most of our last day there on Saturday. Mummy did fancy a walk to the club house Friday teatime but daddy wasn't bothered, mummy was going to ask Storm if she wanted to go but she had her head stuck in a book she'd just bought. So mummy stayed in like billy no mates, I pretended I was asleep so she wouldn't ask me. The plan on Saturday was to go for breakfast at the club house and then have a walk round the lake [or a ride in my carriage pending how tired I was], then we were going to have a few drinks at the pub down the road and go back to the club house. It was said it was going to be a nice day so we were going to sit outside and enjoy the view. Anyway ……. We were getting ready on the Saturday to go for breakfast when mummy noticed it was the 25th, she went into a panic and checked the booking email, yep it was the 25^{th,} Saturday the 25th not Sunday the 25th. So you know what that means? No breakfast, no last day, we're going home! Mummy said she was sorry and kept apologising, she was sure we were going home Sunday and said all week that we were going home Sunday, so how did she get the day wrong? It was the quickest they've ever packed up I'll tell you! Rubbish was taken out, a quick clean round to make it tidy, and a lot of huffing and puffing while packing. I was okay as I was in my bed, then I saw mummy move my food and water dish, then the mat my dishes were on. In all the world Of Princess's did I get a shock when they had to move me out of bed to pack it into the car. Looking back on it all it was quite funny, and they laugh about it now, at the time mummy felt so silly and apologised all day! I did miss the breakfast though as I knew I'd get a sausage or two, opposed to the dog food I got back home!

We had Chinese that night, I was only allowed a few chips, I need to remind them when they have food they need to cater to the needs of one Princess, I just don't know who they think they are!

I forgot to tell you that when we were at the lodge, there were ducks and rabbits everywhere you looked, and a few days when we had the door open, they ventured into the lodge! They didn't bother me, mummy said if Ted was there they wouldn't have made it halfway before he chased them off. But they didn't worry me, I left them alone so they could come in and explore, as long as they didn't go near my food!

When we arrived home, Spike was straight out of his house and came running to the fence, he went crackers when he saw us all, especially mummy. And yes, he came straight round and was with us all day, well til midnight really as his daddy was at a wedding that night and picked him up when he got back. He's hardly been back home since hehehe!

Our next holibobs that was at the end of August for a week to Blackpool has been cancelled, mummy and daddy think it might be too much for me. Blackpool is really busy and there's always so much going off they said I'd not cope with the fast pace of it all and it wouldn't be fair to put me through it. Also, as lovely as the hotel is where we stay it's got lots of stairs and I can't get up them now without help and even then, I struggle. It's not fair on daddy to keep lifting me up as I'm not a small Princess. Thinking about my health and safety at this stage of my life, it's best we stay home and let me rest and enjoy my life, doing what I want to do day by day.

CHAPTER 18

TEDDY TEDDY LISTEN

[There was this one time when ...]

{ White feathers }

Teddy, Teddy, listen, there was this one time when we went to York with Storm to look round her university and we did keep seeing white, feathers, really, we did. They were everywhere. We parked the car in the car park across the road and we went to the toilets, guess what was outside? A white feather! Then we walked across the road to the university and there was a trail of white feathers, all along the path we walked on, all on to the marquee we had to walk through and all through the outdoor part to get round the Uni, it just looked like you had laid out a path for us and you were there with us. Even when we came outside afterwards and it was raining, did we see more white feathers! You were there the whole day Ted and helped Storm make up her mind that's where she wanted to go knowing you were looking out for her.

Teddy, Teddy, listen, there was this one time where a white feather helped daddy make his mind up to change his car for a different one. Daddy didn't really need to change his car but a newer model of his car became available and daddy was umming and arrhing if to change it or not cus he loved his car. Anyway one day, daddy used the newer car to pick Storm up from dance class and while he was waiting for her a white feather landed on the passenger side mirror. This feather stayed there the whole journey home and when daddy called mummy out to show her, she said it was you Teds giving your approval. It turned out daddy did keep the car and it's ended up being cheaper to run. Thanks Ted.

Teddy, Teddy, listen, there was this one time when we went out for a walk and as I was trotting along, did a white feather fall down on to my back! Well mummy was in a tizz, she was so pleased cus we knew it was you showing your approval that I'm their baby girl now. And to top it off, guess what happened after Ted? There was only a white feather on daddy's shoe, really there was! So on that walk you appeared twice, and mummy said it was lovely as she believed it was you and Roxy both together, looking after each other.

Teddy, Teddy, listen, there was this one time when mummy was going next door to pick Spike up and as she opened next doors gate was there a white feather float down! Well mummy said you could have, well knocked her down with a feather! After she had got Spike and she came out of the house, what did she see? What we think it was the same white feather that presumably the wind had blown on to the door step!

Teddy, Teddy, listen, there was one time when we were driving home from wherever we had been on our walk and mummy was upset as she'd not seen a feather that morning. This was the early days of losing you and each time mummy went out there was always a feather somewhere prominent as though you were there. This particular day she hadn't seen one and was abit upset when in all the world of Princess's would you believe, as daddy was driving home did a white feather fall and land on the windscreen of the car! Mummy's day was made after all.

We see white feathers all the time Ted and it's always special to see them, it's more special if it's somewhere we've not been for a while where you loved going. Or if we are talking about you and we suddenly see one, it's always lovely to know your around and looking over me, Ruby. Mummy's so proud of you looking out for me.

{ Daisies }

Teddy, Teddy, listen, there was this one time when, mummy said there was so many daisies in our back garden and she's never seen as many. It turns out you used to eat them, really you did. I'm a clever girl, being the Princess I am, so I told mummy that there's loads of daisies now cus you're not eating them. She's silly cus she didn't realise!

Teddy, Teddy, listen, there was this one time when, we were out for a walk not far from where we live, when I needed a wee wee. I obviously did what I needed to do and you'll never guess what? I only wee wee'd on the one and only daisy that's on the grass! Really, there were no other daisies anywhere on all that stretch of grass and I had to find the only one, I'm a clever girl.

Teddy, Teddy, listen, there was this one time when, we were in the woods and ended up seeing a patch of daisies in the buttercups you used to run through! Do you remember when all the buttercups were in full bloom and you used to charge right through them? There was never a daisy in sight, well this particular time there were loads. Really there was! A massive patch of daisies just for you.

Teddy, Teddy, listen, there was this one time when, we went to the garden centre to get some beautiful flowers / plants for your garden and while we were looking around, we saw some daisies, really, we did! Ok they weren't exactly what you find in the garden but they were practically identical. A team TeddyRoxyRuby member had asked for a daisy plant if we saw one and this was ideal. The stems were longer than a normal daisy but the flower was just the same and just as beautiful so we bought it. We planted it actually in a planting basket and it's perennial so comes back each year, as of writing this it's just starting to bloom now. It's a good job it's off the ground being as you like to eat them.

[Robins]

Teddy, Teddy, listen ,there was this one time in the woods and as I was having my walk with Spike, mummy was walking minding her own business when next thing you know she had a robin fly right in front of her! Really Ted, it was that close mummy felt it fly past her nose! Daddy saw it and was stunned, mummy couldn't believe it and was happy that you were so close to her. The robin flew on the ground and was there for quite a while, mummy cried and said, "hi Ted, love you sausage".

Teddy, Teddy, listen, there was this one time when, we were again in the woods. We walked past your favourite place in the woods which is where there's a dip with a stream at the bottom. Mummy said she always laughed at you as you'd go running down as fast as your legs would take you, have a drink from the stream, then run back up to mummy and daddy with the biggest smile on your face. Only you'd forget your babby! Mummy used to say to you "Ted you forgot your babby, go get your babby" then you'd come running back up again with the babby in your gob. It was definitely your favourite spot in the woods and one day as we walked past we did see a robin on the branch of the tree. That made mummy's day, it stayed there a few seconds then flew off, then flew back again to the branch, mummy said you were teasing her. Maybe that's why you flew near enough in her face before? You were definitely saying hello.

{ Butterflies }

Teddy, Teddy, listen, there was this one time when, Spikes dad next door was having decking on his back garden and a new fence put up. It wasn't long after I'd come to live here and your beautiful garden hadn't been

145

extended so there was only a few bits on it until it got built up. Anyway, cus they have a massive fishpond next door, the fencing and decking that was needed was placed on our back garden as there wasn't room next door. Mummy was upset that your garden had been moved but like I say at that time there wasn't much on it and they held off buying anything else until next doors fence was done.

It took about two weeks til it was all done, and mummy couldn't wait for it to be finished so we could add to your memorial garden. When it was finished, we left a panel of the fence lifted up so we could talk to Spikes dad, Spike was with us on our back garden. In fact, on our garden there was me, [Princess], mummy, daddy, Reece and Storm so we were all outside. What happened next was amazing and in all the world of Princess's it's something you'd never imagine. Did we see the most beautiful purple butterfly, yes Ted, a purple butterfly. We'd never seen one that colour before [or since] it was the same purple as your collar, lead and harness. It was you Ted, we all got goosebumps, each and every one of us, it was like you were saying hello, and asking for the memorial to be put back as it was. The butterfly circled round for about five minutes and we watched in awe, it was beautiful, it was you, it was Ted.

When mummy had put the memorial back as it should be, what did we see? A robin, a robin on the fence, a robin on the fence that hadn't been seen on the fence since the work next door had started. Coincidence? No, we don't think so either.

[Note, the fence the robin was on is our fence at the other side where it always used to sit, not the fence that had just been built next door. The robin visited daily but had disappeared for a few weeks.]

Teddy, Teddy, there was this one time when, we were out on our walk and we were surrounded by butterflies, all of them were brown, some with markings, some plain but all beautiful. Mummy said how lovely it would be if we saw another purple one, we didn't see another purple one but what we did see right in between the brown ones was a red one. What colour did you used to have before you were a purple boy? Yes, that's right, red, you were a red boy.

Teddy, Teddy, listen, there was this one time when, we were once again at the garden centre and choosing some plants / flowers and getting stuff we needed for the garden. When you went to the garden centre you always used to pee pee [I do that now, you'd be proud of me], anyway this particular day I had a pee pee and guess what was flying round me? Yes, a butterfly, and as we were walking round and got to the garden features and the fountains you always had a drink out of, guess what was fluttering on that very fountain? Yes, a butterfly. As we walked round and chose a plant, what landed on that exact plant? Yes, a butterfly. As we went to pay for the trolley of stuff we had, guess what landed on the till? Yes, a butterfly. Okay, so this butterfly wasn't red or purple but oh Ted, it was everywhere we went. Mummy knew it was you, I did too.

We see a lot of white feathers, daisies, robins and butterflies whilst out and about, but the above are just a few examples of times we've been "goosebumped".

Mummy keeps all the white feathers she's collected in a lovely little case she bought and they're all kept safe. We only collect them now 2 years on if there's any meaning behind them like if we go somewhere for the first time since we lost Ted and there's a feather there as soon as we turn up. But they are all very special and very precious.

CHAPTER 19

TEDDY USED TO DO THAT

When I'm out walking and I need to wee wee, I always do it in the same place, on the same stretch of grass, on the same path, in the same bushes, in the same place regardless of where I go or where I am. Teddy used to do that.

When I walk a certain route, which is up towards where Storm's school used to be, there's a small wall, each time I go passed it I have to jump / step over it. Mummy tells me not to each time as it's actually a small wall to someone's garden. Teddy used to do that.

There's a house on our road, I don't really know who lives there, we've seen them come and go but don't really speak. For some reason I always stop at the entrance to the house where the bushes are and have a sniff, I don't know why. Teddy used to do that.

When we go to one of our little countryside places, there's a bridge that takes you obviously to the other side. I'm always curious what's at the other end and most days I tried to walk over, I get called back. Teddy used to do that............. one day I was shocked when I was allowed to go over to the other side and as I walked over, I saw lots of grass and had a toddle through it. Teddy used to do that.

I don't like being told off, or not so much being told off but being told no or I can't do something. My reaction to this is to look at whoever is guilty of telling me and giving them the side eye look. Teddy used to do that.

Sometimes when I look at people, I get called Elvis as I get what they call an "Elvis lip" and it makes them laugh. Teddy used to do that.

When I'm laid down all comfy, I sometimes don't want to move, but if I get rudely disturbed, I let them know about it and expect a belly rub. I'll lift my front paw up so they can tickle in the nook of my chest then lift my back leg up for a belly rub. Teddy used to do that.

If I'm out anywhere, garden centre, pet shop, anywhere I'm allowed to go, I'll make sure to have a wee, well when a Princess needs to go, she really needs to go! Teddy used to do that, when a lad needs to go, a lad needs to go [onest he does].

When I go to the pet shop, I'm expected to walk round all nice and sensible, I might be a Princess now but even a Princess can be a little bit rebellious. It's like expecting mummy and daddy to walk in a pub and not want to get straight to the bar for a drink. How can I be expected to walk round a pet shop without pulling to get to the treats? I get near to where I want to be then have a look, what do I want? What DO I want? Any treat will do? I have a look at what I fancy and help myself to it off the shelf, then I'll lay in the middle of the floor and won't move until I've eaten it all. Teddy used to do that.

I get a lot of attention when I'm out and about, mainly cus I'm beautiful [Teddy used to do that], but sometimes because of my hair. Now, I've no lion mane like Ted had, but I've my own fair share and I do make people jealous as it gets naturally streaked in the sun. My hair goes lighter than the rest of my fur and it's noticeable too, people say, "oooh look at your hair, I have to pay to get mine like that" and I always walk off really pleased with myself. Teddy used to do that.

When people are eating, I like to be sat near them so I get some too, even if I've eaten my own food, well I am a Princess now! I'll sit and wait, and wait, and if it goes on long enough that I don't get anything, I'll start drooling, like proper drooling, my mouth covered and it is dripping on to the floor. Teddy used to do that.

When I'm asleep and I wake up cus people are laughing, I'll lift my head up and look round at them, then they'll say "ooh Rubes you smelly bum" and make out I've farted! I know its them really and they're blaming me, one Princess does not let one rude one off! Teddy used to do that!!!!!!!!

CHAPTER 20

LOVE N STUFF

I never expected my life to turn out like it has, I've been so happy with my family and they love me so much, I never thought I'd ever be so wanted, so loved, so happy. My life expectancy when I got adopted was said to be 13 months or so. As I'm writing this, I'm just short of my two year anniversary or gotcha day. I'm a totally different girl now, I was skinny, now I'm not, I was bald and scabby, now I'm not, I was unloved and unwanted, now I'm not. I'm still on medication for the rest of my life and for ever long that is I know my family are doing all they can for me. I don't go upstairs to bed now but either daddy or mummy stay downstairs each night with me so I'm not on my own. I have trouble getting up off the floor when I've been laid down, it don't help we have wooden floor so that's slippery too, but I do always get up, either on my own or with some help. I'm not in pain, I sometimes get uncomfortable in my back legs but that's Arthur and I don't like him, hehehe I'm teasing you, it's my arthritis.

I always start my walks off by actually walking, I never get straight in my carriage, I do know when I've had enough and daddy will lift me into my carriage and I'll have a rest. After a while I'll get out for another walk as I like to keep myself going. I'll never give up on my life, it's too precious, I was a fighter before, when I was being cruelly bred time after time, I was a fighter when I was cruelly dumped, and I was a fighter to get myself off the streets. So now I've actually got a family who love me and who I love, I'll never give up and they won't let me, they love me too much.

Sometimes when we're out on our walks I'll hear mummy and daddy talking, they'll say how amazing I am, and they'll see the determination on my face. I even have moments of doing things they wouldn't expect me to do, I'll be walking then all of a sudden, I have a spurt and start to speed up, I don't run, but I'll get my legs going and have a toddle off. Or they'll be a little ditch I need to pass and rather than walk round it, I'll do a little jump, that really amazed mummy and daddy, they were talking about that for days and still mention it now when we walk that same way.

I still love my food, and I still spin round and round when I know I'm getting fed, or when someone else is getting fed, as that means I get some too. They still call me Kylie and say I need gold hotpants, even now they laugh how cute I'd look. [Don't get any ideas, there's no way I'd let them do that to me, though I do have the legs for it]

I surprised mummy once, I've been sleeping on my bed in the living room, then one day mummy came into the room and there I am, laid looking all beautiful on the settee! Mummy was so happy, she started near enough screaming and got daddy to come and look at me, he couldn't believe it either. How in all the world of princess's did I get myself up on that settee without any help? I'm not telling!!

I've always got a waggy tail, it never stops, even when I've had to be helped up or down stairs, my tail will still give that wag. When I'm laid down, it sounds like thunder, I'll be laid on my bed and when I see mummy come in the room all you can hear is thud, thud, thud, and that's my tail wagging on the floor. I get called "waggy" sometimes, I'm just such a happy girl, wag, wag, wag. I can multitask too, I'm really clever! You see, when I spin round, I wag my tail too, that's not easy to do but a Princess can do it! And I do like to show off the most beautiful feathers on my tail too, they are so long and pretty. When I first got adopted, I didn't have any feathers at all on my tail, it was just bone and stained yellow, look at me now!

I still have that awful cough too and though it hasn't got any better, it hasn't got any worse and I have learned to live with it. I think it bothers my family more than it bothers me, but again I'm on medication for it and I'm not in pain. I do love taking my meds though as I get some of them wrapped in ham or chicken slices, sometimes I accidently let the tablet fall out of the meat so I have to have another slice …… what? Well a princess must be clever you know!

I want to thank each and every one of you who has taken me to their heart and supported me and my journey. I know I had very big paws to fill after Teddy, and I know we are different, but I'm so glad you all allowed me to take over the running of the TeamTeddyRoxyRuby page and loved me too.

Many thanks for all the cards, presents, and money for special occasions and let's hope they'll be many more. I've come a long way in two years and I couldn't have done it without the love and support of my family, and you, the followers. I love you all.

So, I'm living my life, living the dream, and I'm happy, I'm loved, I'm looked after, I'm fed and don't forget, I'm a princess now.

Love n stuff

Princess Ruby xxxx

Ruby celebrated her 2 year adoption with us on the 19th of June 2024 and had a wonderful day, she was spoiled with so many cards and presents for which we are grateful. Sadly on the 22nd of June, her back legs gave way on her. It was a Saturday and she was still so happy, smiling and wagging her tail even though she struggled to stand up. She could stand with help but couldn't walk very well so we guided her where she needed to be with holding her up. By the Sunday night she was losing control of her bowels but all the time she was still smiling. If Ruby was ever in any pain, she didn't show it, she was smiling through everything and was happy as always.

On Monday the 24th of June, Ruby, with our help managed to get outside on the back garden. She laid on the garden for ages, the sun on her beautiful face and the smile firmly fixed. She got up for a walk round and managed a few steps before losing her balance. By this time I had already rang the vets to see if they could give her pain relief or something for her legs and she was booked in the vets later that day.

After being at the vets all day on pain relief, it was said that the cancer had spread to her legs and had taken over the back legs. We went to the vets hoping to collect Ruby that night but sort of knowing in our hearts we weren't taking her home. When we saw Ruby, she was laid down on her belly and looked so comfortable but we knew it wasn't good. We spoke to the vet and I asked if Ruby could get up and she said no. I begged her to give her some form of injection in her leg to strengthen it so we could give her extra time. I begged her to do

156

something, anything, so we could take her home, pain free. I begged and begged, and begged. I wasn't ready to let my Princess go. This was a repeat of when we lost Teddy and I didn't want to feel that pain again.

There was nothing that could be done. I was already on the floor with Ruby, loving her, stroking her, kissing her beautiful little nose. I slumped even more when I realised we were going to have to say goodbye. Storm and Andy said their own goodbyes and gave her a kiss. I sang our special song to her one last time "Twinkle twinkle little star, Ruby is the best by far, mummy's baby, little girl, oooh I love you all this world, twinkle twinkle little star, Ruby is the best by far".

I held, cuddled and kissed Ruby through masses of tears while she was sadly put to sleep. That pain again was like no other, our Princess, our baby, our girl, our superstar, our Ruby closed her eyes for the last time at 6.45pm 24.6.24.

Princess, we love and miss you so much. We're so happy we adopted you and gave you the life we did, but that don't stop the hurt and this awful feeling of losing you.

RUBY TRIXIE BURGESS WE WILL NEVER EVER FORGET YOU. A TRUE PRINCESS FOREVER, BABY GIRL, WE LOVE YOU.

Rest in peace sweetheart, say hello to Teddy and Roxy and please all 3 of you, look after each other.

Mummy xxxxx

·